EDUCATION & PHILOSOPHY

B
126
.W335
1968

Wang, Gung-hsing

The Chinese mind

DATE DUE

THE CHINESE MIND

GUNG-HSING WANG

THE CHINESE MIND

GREENWOOD PRESS, PUBLISHERS
WESTPORT, CONNECTICUT

Copyright 1946 by Gung-Hsing Wang

Reprinted with the permission
of Doubleday & Company, Inc., Garden City, New York

First Greenwood Reprinting 1968
Second Greenwood Reprinting 1971

Library of Congress Catalogue Card Number 68-23336

ISBN 0-8371-0260-X

Printed in the United States of America

CONTENTS

BOOK II   THE SHIFT TO CONFUCIANISM

BOOK III   THE BEGINNING OF A NEW ERA

PREFACE

THIS IS A STORY of Chinese thought from Confucius to
Sun Yat-sen, covering a period of twenty-five centuries. It
tries to tell the reader what China has been thinking and
how her thoughts have affected her national development
and made her what she is today.

The study of Chinese philosophy has too long been
confined to a restricted number of Sinologists. It is time
that the public take an interest in our thoughts and find
out for themselves just what is implied in the proverbial
notion that China is rich in her philosophy as well as her
wisdom of living.

This little volume is an attempt to interest the English
reading public in our philosophy. I gather the courage to
do it because if the story is told simply and cohesively the
public will want to read it even though it concerns a field
of knowledge far removed from the center of the Occident's usual interest. It must be admitted, however, that
the undertaking is a risky one. For instead of arousing the
interest of the public, I may only succeed in provoking
scholars to criticize my unorthodox way of presentation.

Chinese philosophy has been my hobby for about sixteen years. Written by one who considers it fun to study
the subject, this volume is not intended as a sample of a
serious academic dissertation. Like a narrator reciting the
stories of yore over a teacup, I pick out only those philosophers whom I consider important, interesting, and representative in their respective fields of thought. The main
purpose is to picture the influences of philosophy on the
national growth of China.

A little explanation is necessary regarding the chronological arrangement of the chapters. The reader will notice

that sometimes a philosopher of an earlier period is presented after a philosopher of a much later date. This happens because in the interest of maintaining the sequence of thought the author treats each school of thought as one unit. Within the unit, the chronological order is followed. But when another school of thought is presented, the same arrangement is repeated over again.

The narrative is roughly divided into two parts: the pre-Ch'in philosophers who founded the various schools of thought, and the Confucianist scholars who dominated the scene of philosophy from the Han dynasty (206 B.C.–219 A.D.) to the turn of the present century. Among the pre-Ch'in philosophers, Chapters III to V inclusive deal with Confucian thinkers. Chapter VI illustrates the Taoist school. Chapter VII describes Motzu, an independent thinker of considerable influence. And Chapters VIII and IX present two interesting but unclassified philosophers. The rest of the book follows as closely as possible the style of a chronological narrative.

Transcription and spelling of Chinese names and terms follow the standard Wade-Giles system.

My thanks go to Dr. R. P. McCutcheon, Dean of the Graduate School of Tulane University, for his encouragement.

I am especially grateful to Dr. Hu Shih for his kindness in reading the manuscript and criticizing it. I promise him constant endeavors that the day may come when as a student of philosophy I shall succeed in elevating myself to approximate the high standard he sets for my goal.

GUNG-HSING WANG

Chinese Consulate
New Orleans, Louisiana
January, 1946

I. INTRODUCTION

WORLD WAR II brought to the foreground the importance of ideals in shaping the course of history and the fortunes of mankind. Today, more than ever before, the understanding of what the peoples of the world are thinking will guide us in adjusting our relations with one another and in planning more intelligently a better postwar world order.

Among the United Nations, the one which is least understood by her partners is China. This is naturally so because my country, being culturally and racially different, does not share a common background with the Western world. However, instead of constituting a barrier to understanding, our being different ought to be an invitation to the Occident to try to know us better. After all, modern science has long since made it impossible for us to hide from each other. Now that we must live together in one world, why can't we learn to make the best of it?

Unless the West decides to restrict the one world to the Occident, you must learn to deal intelligently with us. And China, being an important factor in the Orient, should occupy a prominent place in your quest for knowledge.

Personally, I have a feeling that no amount of current information concerning China will enable an American really to understand us without a knowledge of our background. I shall try to explain my country by what we have been thinking in the past and how the traditions and institutions formed by our thoughts have shaped our history and made us what we are today. My position is that ideology has just as much to do with the behavior of a people as the process of thinking has to do with the conduct of an individual.

In tracing the influence of mind over personality development, one does not jot down every little thinking process of an individual. What is more important is to study those mental currents which have left indelible marks in his character or the effects of which have become a part of his individuality. If in the life of an individual there was a period when his mind was clogged with blankness, no point is gained by digging up what he was thinking then. Not that these thoughts are not worth looking into; they have to be skipped because they had little to do with the making of an individual. What is the case with an individual, I try to apply to a nation.

In the chapters to follow, I plan to trace for you those currents of Chinese thought which have left indelible marks in our national growth or have become a part of our national traits. While I am engaged most of the time in discussing the past, I have made it my point not to depart from the present. If it seems that I have written more about our ancient and current philosophy than that of the interim, it is because I restrict my inquiry to those currents in our national thinking which have made us what we are today. I deal only briefly with the philosophy of the Hans, the Weis, and the Six Dynasties; for philosophically speaking, it was a period when our national mind was clogged with blankness.

I do not propose to be a psychoanalyst for the Chinese nation. But by analyzing our national mind and re-evaluating our cultural background, I hope to arrive at a set of conclusions which may be helpful to those who are seeking the betterment of China as a nation and a people. This, however, is merely a wish.

And my prayer is that this little attempt of mine at thought analysis of a nation may be the beginning of a series of really worth-while studies by qualified scholars on the broad subject of Chinese philosophy.

II. THE BIRTH OF CHINESE
THOUGHT

IN MY STUDY of Chinese history I have often observed that our humanistic thinking, more than anything else, has been the determining factor in our way of life. Name anything Chinese, chances are that it is more or less linked with our moral conceptions. In politics, we like to talk about the importance of virtue in the art of government instead of the technique of promoting administrative efficiency. In military science, our thoughts revolve around brotherly love, faithfulness, and mutual trust as superior weapons to heavy armament and trained warriors. Our attitude toward different religions is conditioned by how much good each of them can accomplish rather than limited to the narrow confines of prejudices and persecutions. Regarding literature, we judge its merits by the moral lessons it contributes to the readers. In painting the scenes of nature, it is the artist's ability to absorb the spirit of nature which counts most. It seems that everything concerning China is somehow connected with either the meaning of living or the purpose of life. No one will ever understand us unless he knows first what we have been thinking and how our thoughts have affected our life.

It is a curious thing that China should have concerned herself mainly with humanistic thought for the last four thousand years. More curious still is the fact that even with that much time at our disposal, our people have failed to stumble across science and industrial technique in their search for human knowledge. Is humanistic thinking so strongly rooted in China that it crowds out the growth of other branches of learning? To find the answer, we must go back many thousands of years to the time when the Chinese nation was founded on the banks of the Yellow River.

Ancient as China is, no one knows where the Chinese people came from originally. From evidences which archeologists have dug up in North China, chances are that there were human beings living or roving there long before the known history of China began. For our purpose, it is safe to say that whenever and wherever human beings got together they found occasions to use their heads and hands. As thoughts and deeds began to react on each other, philosophy took root.

In the case of Chinese philosophy, it took root when our concepts of *Heaven* and the *family system* were formed. Long before Confucius our ancestors were already settled in family groups on the banks of the Yellow River. They were ruled by the chiefs of their respective clans. These clans in turn were governed by the chief of the most powerful clan. Those patriarchs, in addition to looking after the needs and welfare of those under their charge, also assumed an over-all control over the affairs, personal or otherwise, of their wards. Each family unit, comprised of persons related by blood, tilled the fields as a unit. Social intercourse among its members was more or less restricted within the family circle. When the patriarch died, those immediately under him devised ways and means of honoring him, and of providing the next in line to succeed him. As time went on, the family system, a unique feature of China's social organization, was gradually evolved. Thus long before any philosopher began to speculate on the functions, obligations, and virtues of our family life, our people were already worshiping their ancestors, respecting their aged, and making the family into the political, economic, and social nucleus of the nation. While it is true that all peoples, Chinese included, evolve their civilized life more or less from tribal patterns, it must be stressed that only in China did this institution of family provide one of the two original foundations on which was later erected the magnificent edifice of their philosophy.

The Chinese concept of Heaven was another important source from which our early philosophers drew heavily for their subject matter. Here again, we recall that our ancestors had become an agricultural people long before the recorded history of China began. Settled on the upper reaches of the Yellow River, they had to adapt themselves to the severe climate of the region. The extreme cold of the winter was only matched by the extreme heat of the summer. Drought and famine took turns in visiting them. They had to rely mainly on their own efforts to make a living. Even then they were at the mercy of nature; for in spite of their efforts, the unpredictable forces of nature could still destroy their crops and render them destitute.

In the course of time what nature could or would not do became the determining factor of life or death. Thus, where human efforts failed, reliance on some sort of supernatural force began. In the case of our ancestors, the predominance of nature over their destiny gradually crystallized itself into a concept of Heaven typically their own.

At the beginning our concept of Heaven was a crude mixture of personal and impersonal aspects. From our ancient records, believed by competent authorities to have been in existence before Confucius, Heaven was sometimes described as an awesome and unfathomable force of limitless space, pouring forth great floods. At other times Heaven was regarded as the source of righteous authority.

The Book of Poetry, for instance, referred to it as the highest ruler governing the people of the four corners to foster their well-being. Many a war which was fought in ancient times was committed in the name of Heaven. In ceremonies preceding a military campaign it was customary for the campaigner to accuse his opponents of violating the *decree of Heaven* and to proclaim himself the one authorized to carry out the punitive powers of Heaven.

The concept of Heaven as developed by our ancestors arose among the ancient peoples of other lands. But with China it is of utmost importance. As my story unfolds, you will see that it has given birth to our peculiar brand of fatalism, our "democratic" ideals, and our religious regard for virtuous living. In fact, throughout our twenty-six centuries of philosophic thinking there is not a single instance where the concept of Heaven failed to enter into the picture.

Chinese humanistic thought was born with the formation of our family system and our concept of Heaven at the beginning of our national life. The former provided us with a basis for regulating relationships between man and man, while the latter inspired us to speculate on the relationships between man and the unknown. Together they have been impelling us onward in our search for a workable formula or set of formulas which will bring forth harmonious human relationships as well as a thorough assimilation of our concepts of value, virtue, the meaning and purpose of life, with "the decree of Heaven."

BOOK ONE

FOUNDERS OF CHINESE THOUGHT

THE CONFUCIANIST SCHOOL

III. CONFUCIUS (551–478 B.C.)

CHINA'S GREATEST TEACHER OF ALL THE AGES

> The way of the Great Learning is to make the virtues shine; to teach and encourage the people to strive for the good till the goal of the supreme good is reached.
> —T'seng-tzu (fifth century B.C.)

CHINA HAD PHILOSOPHY long before Confucius. But among our philosophers he was the first. Many of my countrymen who believe in our ancient history may frown at this observation. The idea that we produced our first philosopher only two thousand and five hundred years ago is hard to swallow. Don't we have a civilized history of almost five thousand years?

I have good reasons in naming Confucius as our first philosopher. Preceding him, there may have been philosophers. Unfortunately they were more legendary than real. Granted that some of them were real, still no one can prove that the books concerning their respective thoughts were actually written by them before the recorded sayings of the Great Sage. Furthermore, Confucius, by compiling all the ancient writings, histories, records, and folklore known to him and incorporating them in his system of thought, was unmistakably the first person in China who started thinking in a philosophic way.

At the time of Confucius, those who wanted to do some thinking never had to be afraid of shortage of materials. Food for thought was plenty.

China was then nominally ruled by an emperor whose authority scarcely reached the outskirts of his capital. The rest of the country was divided into hundreds of feudalistic states, each governed by a prince or a duke. These feudal lords, besides being undisputed masters of their respective domains, fought constantly among themselves, each seeking to encroach upon the wealth and territory of the other. Consequently the whole nation was in an awful mess. The hardships of constant wars imposed upon our people were unbearable. As usually happened in hard times, morality was at a low ebb. Something must be done or the situation would deteriorate beyond repair. Confucius saw enough of this. What he thought was the matter with us started the sequence of our humanistic thinking. To this day the problem of how to conduct ourselves in society still worries us.

Born in 551 B.C. in Shantung, China, Confucius in his seventy-three years of existence was successively a government official, an extensive traveler, an eminent teacher, and a learned editor. He was an ordinary character in every respect, and yet because of it he came to be the most extraordinary personality in all our history.

The background of Confucius, as a descendant of a common aristocratic family, was nothing unusual compared to that of any well-bred Chinese. There were three general classes of people in his day: the princes and dukes who virtually owned their respective domains; their retainers who managed their affairs for them; and the masses who toiled for the two. Confucius was neither lucky enough to be born an owner nor unfortunate enough to be a toiler. His lot, like that of many an educated young man of today, was to do what he could for his country through official channels.

In his younger years our philosopher held offices as tax collector, cattle keeper, etc. Being ambitious and full of ideas, he left his small jobs to look for something big. Traveling extensively throughout China, he campaigned among the various feudal lords for a program of reform. Once he landed a position with the duke of his native state as the royal chancellor. Being too progressive to suit the taste of those with vested interests, he was soon swept out of office. For years thereafter he journeyed hither and thither without much success. Finally when he was around fifty, he gave up campaigning for high offices and devoted seriously his next twenty-three years to tutoring and book editing. With him, life began after fifty, and it proved to be a wise change. By his teachings he perpetuated his ideals for posterity. The succeeding generations, inspired by his thought, have been trying to put his theory into practice ever since. I shall presently tell you what are the damages and the good things which the Confucianists throughout the ages have done to China.

As I look back into our history, I can say without hesitation that no one in China has enjoyed such respect and wielded such influence as Confucius. Among our many philosophers he was by no means the most brilliant. Yet, living as he did an ordinary life, he alone made the biggest hit with our people. Why is it that Confucius attained such an extraordinary position in our country?

I can think of a number of reasons to explain this strange fact. The most important one is that his thoughts are most typical of China. His are what the Chinese like, appreciate, and understand.

In the philosophy of Confucius there is hardly anything which can be called spectacular, unusual, or fanciful. China respects him because his teachings were the results of careful study of the existing idealism of his time. Translating it into such terms as our people could understand, he rooted his ideals deeply in the traditions of our past. This is a sure hit with us; he had the enormous prestige of our ancestors on his side.

Confucius spoke of the Golden Rule as the ideal way of life. It was not just a theory or imagination. As described by him, the Golden Rule was a real thing which actually existed during the ancient reigns of China's wise kings. As the goal of our common endeavors, Confucius taught us to do our level best by reaching or duplicating the Golden Rule of our ancestors. Absurd as it may sound to Westerners, our stagnant civilization is in fact probably a result of the theory, and it suits the Chinese taste perfectly. We love and respect our past. We regard our ancestors with almost religious reverence. How could Confucius miss when he credited the Golden Rule to our ancestors?

An important part of Confucian teachings dealt with family relations. He taught us filial piety, mutual devotion to and affection for one another as the secret to the harmony and happiness of the home. As things were, because of our complicated family organization we had already run into a lot of difficulties in making it work. Wouldn't we be grateful when a wise man like Confucius came along who not only glorified our fundamental institution but also told us in simple and understandable words how to avoid the troubles and to reap abundant happiness therefrom?

Then there is the Confucian fatalism. In the manner of marriage vows in America where the bride is to live happily with her husband for better or for worse and in illness or in health, we are married by Confucius both as a nation and as an individual to the *decree of Heaven*. The idea is that to be happy one must understand fate and be content with it. Do our level best and don't mind the consequences. This sort of fatalism is a great asset to Confucius as it provides him with one-hundred-per-cent protection against possible complaints. Ordinarily, people expect rewards for being good. But suppose that by following Confucian teachings we get raw deals instead. What is going to happen to the Great Sage? By neatly tossing the responsibility of our troubles to fate, Confucius keeps himself clean of all complaints.

There you have my answer to the popularity of China's greatest teacher. Founded on the recognized traditions of our people, his teachings and ideals gave our customs and beliefs the much-needed ideological fortification. What before was a handful of deep-rooted folklore had now become a dignified system of thought. Who, therefore, can be surprised by the profound effect Confucius had on everything Chinese?

What is Confucianism?

As a rule, Chinese terms, being indefinite, are hard to define. Among them Confucianism is the hardest. It looks like a religion, and yet it is not. Its doctrines are firmly believed by our people with almost religious zeal. At one time blasphemy against Confucius and his teachings was punishable by death. As a cultural influence it is probably the steering wheel of our mental and institutional development. Yet in spite of countless numbers of Confucian temples in China, Confucius is decidedly not a god. To our people he is merely "the Most Saintly Teacher." God or the after life is discussed neither by him nor by the scholars after him. Discouraging confession and forgiveness, he simply taught us to be good for the sake of being good.

Leaving the religious issues out, Confucianism still remains to be clarified. The whole body of writings from the *Most Saintly Teacher* to the last Confucian scholar of the nineteenth century can be termed Confucianism. Certain customs and institutions in China which are the causes as well as the effects of Confucianist thought can be termed Confucianism. How shall I tell it to you?

In the absence of a clear-cut definition, the Confucianism which I am about to characterize will be confined primarily to the words of Confucius. Where supplementary clarifications are needed, the notes and writings of his immediate disciples will be used.

The human heart is the basic concern of Confucianism. It is stressed that if our heart is not in the right place, no amount of moral preaching and training will do us any good. The degree of our success in practicing the teachings of Confucius depends on how completely we are able to master our inner self. Tzu-szu, a grandson of Confucius, in summarizing the teachings of his grandfather pointed to the human heart as the basis on which to build Confucian idealism. According to him we were born with intuition and native intelligence which could be developed to the fullest extent for the attainment of the supreme good when driven by a sincere and earnest will.

With the human heart as the origin of the good, Confucianism proposed a three-point program for the individual to follow: Toward the self, the moral goal of a person is to be a chün-tzu or gentleman; toward the family, to be a well-fitting member working for its prosperity and happiness; toward humanity at large, to be an active participant in a world society dedicated to the realization of the Golden Rule.

The first phase of the Confucian moral program is the development of the self. A chün-tzu, as described by Confucius, is "one who sees clearly and hears intelligently, and whose countenance is serene and expression respectful." Continuing, he remarked: "When he [chün-tzu] speaks, he thinks of keeping faith with his words; when he is given responsibility, he thinks of prudence; when he is in doubt, he asks; when he is angry, he introspects; and when he is tempted by profit, he thinks of moral precepts."

On other occasions Confucius described his conception of the gentleman in the following terms:

"A gentleman is one who is slow in words but quick in action. He is known to be filial in his family and brotherly among his friends. His words are faithful and deeds effective. He would rather forsake his life than infringe upon what is right. If it will help establish the good, he does not hesitate to sacrifice his very life."

How to be a chün-tzu? Confucian training, as I pointed out before, begins with the human heart. T'seng-tzu, one of the star disciples, dealt with the subject at length in his book The Great Learning, which has since become a fundamental classic on Confucianism. He believed that all that matters in this world is the knowledge of what a *chün-tzu* should be and how to be one. Basically, he mentioned *mind*, *will*, and *character* as three principal components of a well-developed self. One cannot hope to be a *chün-tzu* unless he sets his mind on the right track. Then with a will fortified by sincerity and earnestness, he proceeds with cultivating a sound character as conceived by the sage.

A person with a weak will but a strong mind is just as unlikely to succeed as one with a strong will but a weak mind. The uphill struggle to attain a Confucian personality implies constant training and strengthening of mind, will, and character. This serious regard for moralistic living and the constant striving for it is characteristic of our people. It is this trait that helps China to retain her conscience in time of stress and strain. And it is this trait which enables a Chinese to regard Christian ethics with benevolent sympathy.

The second phase of the Confucian moral program is to tie the individual securely and affectionately with China's fundamental social institution, the *family*. This theory was so closely and faithfully followed by our people that it gave our country a distinct political structure of its own, one which resembled neither democracy nor the totalitarian state as we know them today. Instead of the state's being subservient to the people as in a democracy, or the people subservient to the state as in a totalitarian country, China subordinated both the interests of the people and those of the state to the interests of the family. It may not be far from wrong to designate China a *"family-cracy."*

Even at the time of Confucius the family had already become the economic, social, and political nucleus of our national life. As a unit it owned, managed, and worked the fields. Of whatever handicrafts existed in the nation, the family was the operating unit. Social contacts seldom exceeded the bounds of family relationships. The ancestral rites which were conducted every now and then kept family solidarity intact. It may be said that the whole country was governed by a myriad of family heads with the emperor at the top as the grand patriarch. Being a practical reformer, Confucius considered it justifiable to use the family, which was already a strong and workable system, as the mechanism for realizing his program of human betterment. In reaching this decision he was not too far wrong. After all, since people spend most of their time with their respective families, why can't this be the best medium for the promotion of human happiness?

According to Confucius the central pivot around which the family system should be built is filial piety. Filial piety, as he conceived it, is not merely to love and honor one's parents. In many ways it is as inclusive as the Christian ideal of love.

While human conceptions of virtue may change from time to time, filial piety seems to have a more stable quality than many of us realize. Because it is tied closely with human nature, we understand its implications far better than those of many another virtue. No parent needs to be taught to love his or her children. Instances occur daily where a parent risks his or her life for the sake of the children. On the part of the children, to love their parents also comes naturally. Likewise the affectionate ties which produce intimate concern over one another's welfare among brothers and sisters are also common in human society. It may take the preacher days, months, or even years to teach us to love one another, with doubtful results. But as to the love which exists among the members of the family, it is more a common reality than an exception.

Confucius saw in filial piety tenderness, care, consideration, and affection for one another. Together these elements made possible a good and full life. Because China is a land of families, because our people are familiar with the sentiments of love which exist within the family, and because that love comprises the essential virtues of a good and full life, he decided that the moral values of filial piety should be the basis of his teachings. If our people could be taught to enlarge the scope of filial love to include all humanity, he reasoned, then the whole world would live as harmoniously and happily as the family.

Thus, in practicing Confucian teachings, the individual lost his identity to the family. Devoting his life to the fulfillment of filial piety, he was assigned definite moral obligations to perform toward his parents, brothers and sisters, children, and relatives. In fact, the theory was later developed to such an extreme that for generations everyone in China was mainly living and working for the family. When the West discovered us in the nineteenth century, we were more family-conscious than nationalist-minded. Lacking in national solidarily but strong in family ties, we found ourselves inadequately prepared to deal with a world dominated by nationalism. Even today our peculiar regard for family ties, which we inherited from our past, still hovers over our heads like a giant pendulum ready to knock us down on our path toward democratization.

The third phase of the Confucian moral program is to make every individual an active participant in the building of a world society. Instead of being just another utopia created by enthusiastic imagination, this ideal is a harmonious order evolved from the conscientious efforts of mankind striving toward its eventual realization. The best exposition on the subject was given by T'seng-tzu, who wrote:

"Those who strive to bring about the Golden Rule in a world society must first put their nation in order. . . . An orderly nation is impossible unless the families within it are well managed. . . . To manage the family well requires a sound character. Sound character implies the presence of mind and the earnestness of will. . . ."

From the foregoing description, it seems that the Confucian world is composed of healthy nations, well-managed families within each nation, and virtuous individuals within each family. It is like an expertly carved Chinese ivory ball where one smaller ball after another is encased in the larger one. Under such a system, each individual is expected to discharge four sets of moral duties simultaneously and constantly. Toward himself, he must strive to cultivate a sound character through the mastery of his mind and will. Toward his family, he must work for its happiness and harmonious relationships. Toward his country, he must contribute to its orderly growth. Finally, toward humanity at large, he must do his part by striving for the realization of a world society exemplifying the Golden Rule.

What is the Confucian Golden Rule? In defining the ultimate goal of his democratic doctrines, Dr. Sun Yat-sen, founder of our republic, often quoted a description which appeared in *The Book of Rites*, an ancient Confucian classic written after Confucius but claimed to be of pre-Confucian origin. Inasmuch as the description paints quite a vivid picture of the state of affairs under the Golden Rule, I quote:

"When the Golden Rule shall finally prevail, the world will belong to all. They will elect the virtuous and the able to take charge of affairs. There will be mutual trust and neighborliness. People will not only love their own parents and look after their own children but the aged will find happiness during their remaining years; the able-bodied will be usefully employed; the young will be properly brought up; the weak, the widowed, the maimed, and the crippled will be taken care of. The men will have what they want. The women will have their mates. There will be such a plenty of commodities everywhere that people no longer will find it necessary to own them. Work will be so common and spontaneous that no longer will one care to labor for his own gain. Conspiracies and disorders will disappear forever together with robberies, thefts, and other crimes. This is the Golden Rule."

A more direct source of the definition can be found in *The Great Learning*, written by Tzu-szu, Confucius' grandson, who said:

"The way of the 'Great Learning' is to make the virtues shine, to teach and encourage the people to strive for the good till the goal of the supreme good is reached."

The Confucian Golden Rule is somewhat similar to Plato's theory of making virtue the center of human activity. While stressing the importance of fitting the individual properly into the idealistic structure of the whole, it also advocates a system resembling the modern version of social democracy. What baffles our people, however, is the failure of the Confucian thinkers to define specifically what they mean by the *supreme good* which is to be the final goal of human endeavors.

In spite of the ambiguous way in which the Confucian Golden Rule was presented, certain general principles were laid down to provide us with a basis for speculation. Among them I shall mention two: one, shu 恕 or reflective love as the sustaining virtue of the world society, and the other, knowledge with which to strive for the eventual realization of world brotherhood.

The Chinese character 恕, pronounced shu, is composed of two parts: 如 and 心. 如 means same while 心 means heart. Together it means consistent with conscience. In the absence of a better English equivalent, I call it reflective love, which means love reflected from one's conscience.

Confucius defined shu both positively and negatively. In a negative sense he said: "What you do not wish others to do unto you, don't do it to others." Speaking positively, he said: "What you wish to do for yourself, do it to others. . . . Help others as you would help yourself." He did not speak of "doing unto others as you want others to do unto you," because he thought that one's own conscience should be the origin of good deeds.

The Great Sage apparently attached a good deal of importance to reflective love. One day, wanting to find out how much his disciples understood his ideals, Confucius turned casually to T'seng-tzu, who happened to be nearest to him, and asked: "Can you think of one word which will summarize my teachings?" To which T'seng-tzu replied, "Yes, it is shu practiced with faithfulness." At another time, disciple Tzu-kung asked Confucius, "Will you give me one word to practice the rest of my life?" "Yes," responded the teacher, "the word is reflective love."

Shu is the sustaining virtue of the world society because it provides a common moral basis for our dealings with one another. If individuals and nations will treat one another in the same way as they treat themselves or want themselves to be treated, then, instead of entangling ourselves with perpetual differences, we may accomplish something constructive toward a harmonious world order.

What reflective love is for the heart, knowledge is for the mind. As the key to true wisdom, knowledge is the tool with which the ethical edifice of Confucianism is built.

What is knowledge and how do we proceed to acquire it? In *The Great Learning* disciple T'seng-tzu wrote:

"To secure knowledge is to study matter. When matter is studied, knowledge results."

By casual observation, the Confucian definition of knowledge sounds almost like that of modern science which, as we understand it today, is the discovery of general truths or of the operation of general laws relating to the physical world. But the catch in the Confucian conception is that nothing can be considered as knowledge unless it contributes toward the realization of the *supreme good*. Thus Tzu-szu, grandson of Confucius, wrote:

"Truthfulness is the way of Heaven; to seek truthfulness is the way of man. . . . To seek truthfulness, one must choose that which is good and attach himself to it; learn extensively; question discriminatingly; think carefully; differentiate thoroughly; and practice faithfully."

It is evident, therefore, that our conception of knowledge is narrowly confined to the study of the spiritual well-being of the individual. Overpowered by the Confucian theory of knowledge, it is no small wonder that our scholars throughout the ages were more concerned with research in human relations than in scientific study of the laws of the physical world.

Wang Yang-ming (1472–1528 A.D.), a famous philosopher of the Ming dynasty, once experimented seriously on the Confucian formula of knowledge. He wanted to find out in what ways knowledge would come from the study of matter. In his bamboo garden he got himself a chair. Sitting there for three days and nights, he watched the bamboo, and looked for it to give forth knowledge. In spite of his wisdom, he was unable to learn anything worth while from the bamboo that could enrich his soul. In this predicament, he concluded that what Tzu-szu meant by studying things was to apply our heart and mind to everything we encountered. What was learned therefrom would be true knowledge.

I can't see anything wrong in the Confucian assertion that knowledge is the key to the eventual realization of a world society. But there are many Chinese patriots who think otherwise. They argue that during the last one hundred years China has been suffering much at the hands of the imperialist powers. All this is due to the fact that we know less about science and technology than the West does. Hence the Occident is "advanced" while we are "backward." This might not have happened if Confucius and his followers had been less insistent in stressing that aside from the subject of virtuous living nothing is worth knowing. As it is, our scholars have been dominated so much by ethical motives in their search for knowledge that they are unable to see anything worth while beyond the moral horizon. Consequently the inventive genius of the Chinese race has been sidetracked, and of science and technology we know no more than our ancestors did in the days of yore. To open the way for materialistic progress, so they advocate, China must free herself completely from the Confucian bondage, the earlier the better.

In thus criticizing Confucianism, our patriots virtually agree with the Great Sage that only virtuous living is knowledge. Otherwise, why must we discard it in order to enlarge our mental outlook? As a matter of fact, the knowledge which we inherit from our ancestors regarding the meaning and purpose of life is just as important as the knowledge about the enrichment of life which we are now learning from the West. A combination of the two will do more for us than can either of them separately.

What remains to be discussed is China's peculiar brand of fatalism as conceived by Confucius and his followers. Occupying an important position in the Confucian system of thought, it goes far beyond the ordinary stoic attitude toward pain or pleasure, adversities or blessings.

Fatalism, to the Confucianists, is a natural condition of life from which no human being is capable of escaping. As a part of the universe man is subject to the same influence which moves the heavenly bodies, regulates the four seasons, and gives this earth the intricacies of life. Against this influence there is nothing a man can do to alter its course. Its subsequent application to the individual or to the family or to the nation is known as the "heavenly fate."

During one of Confucius' extensive journeys his life was threatened by a bandit. After having made his escape, the teacher said to his disciples: "Heaven bestows virtue upon me; what can the bandit do?" On another occasion Confucius was surrounded by a mob mistaking him for a local hoodlum. Somehow they discovered his identity before damage was done. Commenting on the incident, Confucius remarked: "When Heaven is not ready to take me, what can the mob do?" There you have an example of the "heavenly fate" as something predestined and beyond the control of man.

Omnipotent as is the influence of heavenly decree on the individual, yet toward it man cannot appeal for help. One day, a disciple asked Confucius: "Do you ever pray to Heaven?" "If I have erred against Heaven," he answered, "what is there to pray for?" Apparently, the practical thing to do is to correct our past faults and to strive continuously for improvement in our moral stature. "Crying over spilled milk" or asking "forgiveness from a superior source" seems to be an admission of moral weakness which should not be encouraged. "A true gentleman [chün-tzu]," said Confucius, "follows the heavenly dictate and enjoys his fate."

Confucian fatalism has a curious sedative effect on the Chinese tempo of life. Everyone seems to believe that his destiny is more or less controlled by fate and that it is futile for him to struggle against it. As a result he is less jumpy and provocative and learns to adapt himself to what is coming to him in a nonchalant and indifferent manner. While this tends to slow down our life to an easygoing level, it also makes us irresponsible. The thought seldom occurs to us that we can improve the lot of each individual by doing something collectively. Unless this lack of interest in public welfare is corrected, it will continue to constitute a stumbling block on our path of democratic progress. On the other hand, barring its collective implications, fatalism has certainly made many a happy and contented individual out of us; some in a fool's paradise, and others in an atmosphere of real understanding of the meaning of life.

Confucian fatalism also has a paradoxical angle which in a pinch can generate magnificent strength in our people. Because "heavenly fate" can control men, and men on their part have no say about it, we have developed an amazing ability to hold on to our destiny with unflinching determination when threatened with serious crisis. The history of China is full of instances where individuals would rather endure all sorts of torture than to say "surrender" to the enemy. And the people would rather die like ants than quit fighting for what they believe to be their destined fate.

In the field of humanistic thought fatalism has made two important contributions to Confucianism. First, it prepares us psychologically to differentiate the good and the bad from reward and punishment. "Life or death is a matter of fate," said Confucius, "and to be rich or poor is up to Heaven." We are taught not to assume that by being good we will be rewarded and that by being bad we will be punished. Virtue is absolute and must not be adulterated by material considerations. Second, where the element of fate is involved, it strengthens our devotion to moral obligations. "When you are tempted by something profitable, think of moral obligations," warned Confucius. Thus, whenever and wherever we are confronted by a choice between materialistic gains and moral responsibility, we prefer to stake our all with the latter. By identifying our rise or fall with moral values as our predestined fate, we have been able to face the several critical periods in our long history including the present one with a degree of tenacity probably unrivaled by the peoples of other lands. Didn't Confucius say, "A true superior man is he who gives his life to aid the cause of righteousness"?

IV. MENCIUS (372–289 B.C.)

FOUNDER OF CHINESE DEMOCRACY

In the days of Mencius the feudal lords were only
interested in outdoing one another in diplomatic
intrigues. They considered war to be good and desirable. And Mencius, preaching the virtues of the
ancient rulers, found no one in power to agree with
him. He had to retire and teach the doctrines of
Confucius.

—Szu-ma Ch'ien (145–85 B.C.)

ON THE ALTAR of every Confucian temple in China are in-
scribed the names of Confucius and his more illustrious
disciples. Next to Confucius, "the Most Saintly Ancient
Teacher," is Mencius, whose title is "the Almost As
Saintly." In a land where priority in birth usually decides
the order of reverence, it is a strange fact that Mencius,
who studied under a disciple of the grandson of Confucius, should take precedence over many an immediate disciple. An inquiry into the life of Mencius reveals certain
factors which compel our people to respect him.

Aside from having an almost identical career with Confucius, Mencius was the first scholar in China who instilled
the democratic spirit into our humanistic thought and inspired our adherence to virtuous living by making us realize the innate goodness of our nature.

Born in 372 B.C. in Confucius' native province of Shantung, Mencius duplicated in many respects the life of the
Great Sage. This enhanced considerably our esteem for
him. Like his predecessor, he came from a scholar-family,
the symbol of respect in China. Fired by a similar desire
to unite the different warring states into one nation, he
traveled extensively throughout the country preaching his
political and ethical idealism before the different princes
and dukes who were then the actual rulers of China. Met
by similar failure, he retired and taught his followers those
ideals which he had believed and labored for. He died in
289 B.C. at the age of eighty-four. Thus, while other disciples preceding him may have written more about the
teachings of the Great Sage, it was Mencius who not only
made academic contributions but also tried as hard as
Confucius to convert them into reality.

As the first exponent of Chinese democratic thought,
Mencius told our rulers as early as the third century B.C.
that the right to govern was dependent upon the consent
of the people. Realizing that our respect for the decree of
Heaven was already deeply rooted, he made the point that
it was through the will of the people that we learn of the
dictate of Heaven.

As an illustration, I like to present a record of a conversation between Mencius and his friend Wan-chang concerning "the Age of Golden Rule," where the method of
determining the decree of Heaven was explained. According to Chinese history, the Age of Golden Rule took place
sometime between 2357 and 2255 B.C. The story, originally told by Confucius, was to the effect that King Yao,
by his illustrious and virtuous rule, succeeded in making
his people happy. When the time came for him to choose
a successor, instead of giving the throne to his son he ab-

dicated in favor of Shun, the ablest and the most virtuous man of his realm. Confucius was fond of telling this story because he wanted his listeners to realize that the right to govern was a sacred trust and that it should be determined by virtuous qualities instead of birth. Although the Great Sage had since come and gone, the subject continued to interest thoughtful scholars, for the hereditary feudal lords of China were as vicious and unmindful of the people's welfare then as they had been in the days of Confucius. So we find Mencius and Wan-chang discussing the subject with great enthusiasm.

Wan-chang opened the conversation: "Is it true that King Yao gave his throne to Shun?"

Mencius: "No, a king has no right to give away his throne to anybody."

Wan-chang: "But Shun ascended to the throne, didn't he? Who else could have given it to him?"

Mencius: "Heaven."

Wan-chang: "Did Heaven so decree?"

Mencius: "No, Heaven can't talk. One must listen by observing the trend of events and human deeds."

Wan-chang: "How?"

Mencius: "Yao recommended Shun to Heaven as his successor. Heaven approved it because the people accepted Shun as their ruler."

Wan-chang: "Please clarify the procedure once more."

Mencius: "When Yao died, he wanted Shun to succeed him. Shun refused and fled to the country in favor of Yao's son. But the officials of the realm continued to seek counsel from Shun. The people continued to praise Shun. These are signs of heavenly decree as revealed through deeds and events among men. Let me quote you a passage from the ancient classic: 'Heaven sees what the people see and hears what the people hear.' This is what I have in mind."

Lest his disciples fail to perceive the essence of his political thought, Mencius often repeated to them: "People first, the state next, and the least important is the king." Being unafraid to make his popular views known even to the kings, Mencius was one day talking to Prince Ch'i about the justifiability of dethroning rulers by force. They spoke of an ancient dictator-king in our history who was driven from his throne by the people because of his despotism and cruelty. Presently the Prince asked: "Do you consider it justifiable to revolt against a king?" Without hesitation Mencius answered: "When a king treads on virtue and throws away his moral obligation, he is no longer king but an ordinary individual. While no one has the right to harm his king, anyone can kill an undesirable individual."

Besides his being a theoretical exponent of popular rights, we find a number of instances in *The Book of Mencius* describing our philosopher as the champion of the people's well-being.

During one of his extensive tours Mencius was received by the Prince of Liang. After the audience, the potentate took the philosopher to visit his royal garden. Standing by the lily pond, both of them watched the swans, deers, and flowers with interest. The Prince, who had just been told of the importance of moral courage as a prerequisite to good deeds, decided that this was an opportunity to change the subject. Turning to Mencius, he asked, "Does a sage like you also enjoy scenes like these?" Sensing the implication, Mencius answered, "Sire, only a sage can really enjoy this." Continuing, the philosopher explained: "There is an old song which the people are still singing today praising the garden of King Wen, the ancient sage. The words are: 'King Wen wanted a garden. The people built him one. There were deers and swans; fish of all kinds. Blooming everywhere were flowers and precious plants. Both people and king played there. Together, they had a wonderful time.'" Turning to the Prince, Mencius said: "Sire, happiness comes only when you share your joy with the people."

Mencius believed not only that the happiness of the people should be the principal concern of the rulers, but that in promoting it the latter ought to follow the dictate of public opinion. *The Book of Mencius* tells of a visit the philosopher had with the Duke of Ch'i. In the course of their conversation, the Duke wanted Mencius to teach him how to test the loyalty of his officials. Mencius said, "It is more important to select the virtuous to serve you than to dismiss the unfaithful ones." By this the philosopher meant that if the virtuous were given the official position, the question of unfaithfulness would not have arisen. To satisfy the Duke, Mencius continued: "When those around you tell you that so and so is virtuous, the information can be wrong. When your officials tell you that so and so is virtuous, that, too, may be doubtful. But when your people say that so and so is virtuous, then investigate and if he is found qualified, employ him. As to the unfaithful ones, listen only to the advice of the people. When they say that so and so deserves death, investigate and if he is found guilty, execute him." While this lengthy advice might sound unconstitutional to American jurists, Mencius certainly made plain as early as the third century B.C. the importance of public opinion in the affairs of government.

Mencius' simple views on government probably contributed more to the formation of China's basic governmental structure than the ideals of many another philosopher. For centuries our version of "democracy" seemed to follow his line of thought. Believing that the decree of Heaven was the principal influence which controlled the destiny of our nation, we regarded the will of the people as its tangible expression on earth. Consequently the main function of the government was to foster the well-being of the people by entrusting the duties of administration to the virtuous. And when a given dynasty betrayed the heavenly trust by bringing unendurable hardships and sufferings to the people, it was the latter's right and obligation to destroy it on behalf of Heaven.

During the past two thousand years China has more or less followed the political pattern woven by Mencius. In contrast to the unbroken line of emperors in Japan, China has had as many changes of dynasties as were warranted by the feelings of the people dictated by the pressure of living. Throughout our history, the life of an imperial line seldom lasted more than three hundred years. The right to revolt not only made our rulers mindful of the interest of the people but also kept our nation politically virile and dynamic.

"Government by the virtuous," a doctrine introduced by Confucius and reiterated by Mencius, was responsible for the formation of our "scholar rule" system in the second century B.C. By assigning official positions to the Confucian scholars who had successfully passed a series of competitive examinations, it gave the world's first civil service to the Chinese people. Excluding the events of the last century, which I shall explain toward the end of the book, China virtually held the world's record for political stability and orderliness. From "scholar rule" also derives our respect for scholarship, as well as a peculiar brand of authoritarian mentality of the scholars toward the people, both of which will be described in the course of the book. Suffice to say, it seems that a large part of our political tradition can be traced to the democratic thinking of Mencius.

It has often been asked of me: "Since China developed democratic thought at such an early date, why is it that up to now her people still do not know how to govern themselves?"

In my study of European history, I have the impression that the growth of representative government in the West is largely prompted by the fact of excessive oppression on the part of the rulers. The burden was so heavy on the people that they found no relief other than to take the arduous task of government into their own hands. The Magna Charta of the thirteenth century probably would not have resulted had it not been for the despotic and irresponsible conduct of King John. So, perhaps, was the development of the political thought of Montesquieu and Rousseau a product of the feudalistic despotism of Europe. The Chinese people, to the contrary, had not found it necessary to learn to govern themselves. The political doctrines of Mencius gave our national body politic an essentially democratic nature. Our rulers, by adhering to the will of the people, had little opportunity to abuse us. And the system of "scholar rule," a government by the educated and the professionals, assured our people a reasonable amount of administrative efficiency and benevolent regard for their well-being. It seems strange that our democratic traditions spoiled our people and made them unmindful of representative government. But then, many a rich man's son who was born with a silver spoon in his mouth never wanted to be bothered with the art of making a living.

As an ethical thinker Mencius made some outstanding contributions to our understanding of the purpose of life. First to teach the innate goodness of human nature, he made us realize that to live a virtuous life and to be good to one another was the natural course of man prescribed by Heaven. Lest we falter, he added the doctrine of Yi (義), or the moral duty to pursue virtuous living according to the Confucian code by placing moral values above our individual existence.

On the subject of human nature, we find in *The Book of Mencius* the following record of a conversation between the philosopher and his friend Kao-tzu:

Kao-tzu: "Human nature may be compared to flowing water, which can be made to flow eastward or westward. Because it is as flexible as the flow of water, human nature is neither good nor bad."

Mencius: "It is true that water can be made to flow toward one direction or another. But can you make it flow upward? Just as the nature of water is to flow downward, so is the nature of man essentially good. Of course, by arbitrary means you can make the water reverse its natural course. But this is against the nature of water. Similarly, human nature can be made to turn toward evil. That, too, is influenced by environment and cannot be considered its true nature."

The argument used by Mencius to prove his point is true to form in Chinese philosophical writings: straight assertion based on direct observation. Aside from this, the foregoing conversation is of interest to us because it reveals

Mencius' way of thinking. By comparing human nature to water, Kao-tzu merely pointed out that there were certain qualities in the former which reminded him of the latter. But Mencius approached the problem from an entirely different angle. To him the flow of water in a given direction was a phenomenon demonstrating to us what it can do. But when he told Kao-tzu that water cannot flow upward unless by arbitrary methods, the philosopher went beyond its superficial display by perceiving what appeared to him its true nature. In the case of human conduct, Mencius wanted us to view the subject matter not merely from what man can do or can be made to do but by going to the root of the problem through the study of man's original nature.

In order that we may follow Mencius' thought, the reader is urged to assume a traditional Chinese frame of mind by accepting the philosopher's authoritarian assertion that human nature is innately good. Then you will enjoy the way his theme was unfolded. Let us first take from *The Book of Mencius* a sample of his many assertions on the subject:

"All men have the quality of mercifulness, of the sense of honor and shame, of respectfulness and of knowing the right from the wrong. But to discover these qualities, we must keep on searching for them. Otherwise, they will be lost to us forever."

Granted that we are capable of being good because our nature is innately good, the following story on our negligence, taken from the same book, will interest you:

One day Mencius and his disciples walked by a barren field dotted with tree stumps. Comparing it with human nature, he pointed it to the disciples and said: "A virgin forest once grew on this field. Think how beautiful a sight it was then. Now it is only adorned by a bunch of ugly stumps. The rich earth that once nourished the forest is here. The rains and sunshine that once made the trees grow have not changed. But where is the beautiful scene? Axes have cut down the trees, and animals have chewed away the seedlings. Now hear ye! Just as this field possesses the capability of growing beautiful trees, so can human nature generate good deeds. But instead of nourishing it continuously, we let our evil desires abuse it. If we keep up with this foolishness, our character will be as barren and ugly as this field!"

Resting on the thesis that we are capable of being good because our nature is innately good, Mencius concluded:

"We must remember that in spite of our innate goodness, nothing will grow unless it is properly cultivated and nourished. Otherwise, no matter how good is our original nature, without nourishment it will eventually wither."

This logically leads us to a discussion of "nourishment." How are we to nourish our original good nature so that from it will grow a great moral stature?

Mencius seemed to see a difference between goodness as a cause and goodness as an effect. The innate goodness of human nature, for instance, is goodness as a cause because it possesses all the essences which constitute a great moral stature. But cause alone cannot produce effect unless it is set in motion. It is said in the West that mighty oaks from acorns grow. The remark will be true provided the acorns are planted and given the chance to grow. Otherwise, even though possessing all that is needed to develop into a mighty tree, an acorn remains a tiny seed as long as the life within stays dormant. On the other hand, whatever sprouts forth from the fountain of goodness in our nature, be it a thought, a word, or a deed, is goodness as an effect. Our moral stature is measured by how much effort we put in to develop our innate goodness and how much concrete good we are able to realize from it. The moral force which is behind this process is called Yi (義). Remarked Mencius:

"As goodness is the way of human hearts, so shall Yi be the way of human deeds."

Yi therefore implies a moral faith in the goodness of our nature and a moral duty in adhering to virtuous living as our purpose in life.

Because our innate goodness is endowed by Heaven and because it is Heaven's decree that we develop it to its fullest stature, Mencius believed that the pursuit of Yi, our lifelong adherence to virtuous living, should be placed above our very life. He said:

"I love my life. I also love Yi [virtuous living]. But if I cannot have both, I'll forego my life and adhere to Yi. There are things which are more valuable than life itself. One just cannot hold on to his life too much. While it is true that we all hate to die, remember also that there are things which are worse than death.

"Should one's desire to live be stronger than his will to pursue Yi, then any deed which preserves life will be committed in preference to moral values. Likewise, if we allow our fear of death to possess us, what wouldn't we do to escape death?"

To place the value of moral principles above that of life is not an easy thing to do. It requires a condition of mind to brace our will against all kinds of weakening influences. This condition of mind, according to Mencius, is fortitude. He remarked:

"I know how to cultivate fortitude. . . . It is my great-

est and strongest weapon. With it I nourish my conscience.
. . . And its essence of righteousness fills heaven and
earth.

"The world is my home. The good is my way. If I have
the opportunity to carry out what I believe, I will share it
with everyone. If, unfortunately, I am not understood by
my fellow men, I simply carry out my belief alone.

"Wealth and power cannot corrupt me. Poverty and
lowliness cannot change me. Brutal force cannot coerce
me."

Through such strong expressions Mencius conveyed his
faith in the absoluteness of the good which could be
shaken neither by adverse circumstances, discouraging environment, outside p essure, public indifference, nor brutal
might. Many of our scholars, in living up to his standard,
displayed remarkable integrity, poise, and fortitude in face
of danger to their lives, actual or implied, when confronted
with a choice between betrayal or adherence to moral
principles. Invariably they preferred death to compromis-
ing their integrity. As shown in our history, time and again
when crisis envelops China, we have been fortunate enough
to produce leaders of the caliber described by Mencius
whose moral strength and impregnable will defy all obstacles, and through whose exemplary conduct the rest of
us are inspired to uphold the inviolability of our national
integrity in spite of periodic setbacks.

There was Su-wu (140–60 B.C.), for instance, who as an
ambassador to the Tartars in the first century B.C. succeeded in subduing them by sheer strength of character.
Regarded by many historians as our greatest diplomat, by
his moral fortitude he contributed in no small measure toward saving China from Tartar invasion for more than a
thousand years to come. It was not until the thirteenth

century that they again overran our land. From what our historians told of Su-wu, he was commissioned by the emperor to pacify the Tartars, bringing with him a group of Tartar dignitaries whom we had captured during their numerous raids on our border. Upon his arrival at the Tartar capital, somewhere in Outer Mongolia, a series of tortures instead of good will awaited him. First put in a dungeon without food and water, then exiled to what is now Lake Baikal in eastern Siberia, he endured sufferings and privations without asking once for mercy or permission to surrender as demanded by his torturers. To the contrary, disregarding insults to his physical person, never for once did he relapse in his loyalty to his emperor or in upholding the dignity of his ambassadorial position. At the end of the nineteenth year of torture the Tartar chieftain, finding Su-wu still clinging reverently to his imperial credentials, finally broke down himself and returned our hero to China with honors and a solemn pledge never to violate our border again. It was a case where the torturer was subdued by the tortured.

Then there was Yüeh-fei, a scholar-general of the eleventh century, who, by successfully resisting the Chin invasion against overwhelming odds and finally by sacrificing his life for the principles he held dear, personified China at her very best—regarding the preservation of moral values as absolute and above all considerations. At that time the Chin tribesmen from Manchuria had broken through our Great Wall, captured successively two of our emperors, and conquered most of China north of the Yellow River. With our back to the Yellow Sea, with our emperor seeking refuge in Hangchow on the eastern coast, and with our officials actively working for capitulation, General Yüeh-fei prevailed upon the emperor to allow him to organize an army with the sole purpose of restoring our lost territories and driving the invaders back to where they came from. Sabotaged by traitors and battling an enemy superior both in number and quality, he nevertheless pressed on. Just when he was successfully forcing the invaders to retreat northward, the rotten officialdom, fed full of enemy bribes, ordered Yüeh-fei to withdraw in the name of the emperor and to face trial for treason. Our scholar-general, instead of relying on his armed might and military prestige to declare himself independent of the emperor, obeyed and returned with his staff with full knowledge of the plot. While being kept in prison, he and his subordinates were summarily murdered by the traitors. But to the succeeding generations of Chinese, Yüeh-fei died worthily and properly. By resisting the invader in spite of obstacles both from within and without and by remaining loyal to his emperor until death, we consider him to have observed with Yi the absoluteness of moral values and fulfilled his "heavenly destiny."

Toward the last quarter of the thirteenth century the Mongol hordes led by Kublai Khan, grandson of Genghiz Khan, overran our country. There amid despair and hopelessness Wen T'ien-hsiang, the prime minister of China, fought the conquerors for eight long years, the first five with his troops and the remaining three as a prisoner. His character incorruptible, his will unconquerable, and his faith in his country unshakable, he preserved unto death our precious tradition of "China forever." His army was nearly annihilated by the Mongols on several occasions, yet after each defeat he always managed to rise again with a new one. Once he and his whole family were captured. Forsaking his loved ones in preference to his country, he made his escape and emerged with another group of partisans to keep up the fight. It was indeed a war to the finish. When Wen was finally captured in the fifth year of his resistance, Kublai Khan, who despised the conquered as much as he respected the unconquerable, offered him the prime-ministership of the mighty Mongol empire. This he declined. Hoping that good treatment, comfort, and ease might soften him, the chivalrous Khan confined his captive in luxurious surroundings for three years. At the end of the period the Mongol emperor, still clinging to his hope of converting Wen, ordered the prisoner to be brought before him and said: "Tell me your wish and it shall be fulfilled." "Grant me death," responded the ex-prime minister of China. To this day many of our scholars still love to recite a poem by Wen which expressed beautifully his devotion to moral principles. He wrote:

> Ever since the beginning of time,
> Can you tell me who never died?
> Then why not leave this pure heart of mine
> To compete forever with the blue of the sky!

This tradition of the inviolability of moral principles is not restricted to the ancients exclusively. A recent characteristic illustration can be found in the spiritual stamina displayed by Generalissimo Chiang Kai-shek when he was forcibly held by a group of insubordinates in 1936, an event known to the Western newspaper world as "the Sian kidnaping affair." Less than one year prior to the Japanese invasion of 1937, the incident struck China during her greatest crisis in history—dissension from within and impending conquest from without. Just at that time when the leadership of the Generalissimo was most urgently needed, he was "detained" by Marshal Chang Hsueh-liang, an impatient subordinate who believed that he could impose his political views on his superior at the point of a gun. Isolated and surrounded by almost half a million unruly troops, the Generalissimo, by his strength of character, not only convinced the Young Marshal of his mistaken patriotism and made him follow his superior voluntarily to Nanking to face trial, but by so doing turned China's darkest hour into the beginning of dawn. The following words taken from the Generalissimo's diary written at Sian in which he reprimanded the Young Marshal show vividly Chiang's adherence to our ancient tradition of the inviolability of moral values:

". . . According to military discipline and the law of the land, you, as a rebel, deserve not only reprimand but also punishment. My head may be cut off, my body may be mutilated, but I must preserve the honor of the Chinese race and must uphold law and order. I am now in the hands of you rebels. If I allow the honor of the 400,000,-000 people whom I represent to be degraded by accepting any demands in order to save my own life, we should lose our national existence. Do you think that by using force you can compel me to surrender to you rebels? Today you have lethal weapons; I have none, but instead I am armed with principles of righteousness. These are my weapons of defense. . . . I shall do nothing to betray the trust imposed on me by the martyrs of the Revolution. I shall not bring shame and dishonor to this world, to the memory of my parents, and to the nation. . . ."

Thus among the treasure of China's ancient traditions our faith in the absoluteness of moral values, initiated by Mencius and made immortal by deeds of subsequent scholars, stands out prominently as the rudder of a ship steering our nation through many storms.

V. HSÜNTZU (360–230 B.C.)

THE PRACTICAL CONFUCIANIST

*Among the Confucianist scholars of his time, Hsüntzu
alone founded an aggressive school of thought.*
—Hu Shih

AMONG CHINA'S EMINENT philosophers of the Confucian
school, the one who dares to differ from the Great Master,
to speak his own mind, and to think most originally is
Hsüntzu. By reading the three hundred and twenty-three
essays which he left behind, a student of today can still
feel the vigor, the hardheadedness, and the simplicity with
which the philosopher propounded his views.

Born around 360 B.C. when Confucian thought was beginning to enjoy popularity among our scholars, and having himself studied under the disciples of Confucius,
Hsüntzu was little affected by such well-established dog-
mas as the omnipotence of the heavenly fate, the idealiza-
tion of the past, and the innate goodness of human nature.

In contrast to the Confucian theory that men cannot
escape from the influence of the heavenly fate, and that
men's sphere is to do what is humanly possible, leaving the
consequences to Heaven, Hsüntzu not only denied the existence of fate but maintained that human efforts alone
are capable of overcoming all obstacles and of accomplish-

ing our righteous objectives. Arguing that only the way of man should govern human activities, he wrote:

"Heaven will not abolish winter just because mankind does not like cold weather. Nor will Earth shrink in size because we object to long distance. . . .

"As long as we practice thriftiness and enrich the sources of our wealth, Heaven is powerless to make us poor. Likewise, Heaven can hardly make us sick if we nourish ourselves well, take proper care, and exercise regularly. . . .

"Now, were we to neglect our resources while spending lavishly besides, could Heaven make us rich? . . . Would Heaven protect our health should we neglect our nourishment and sit idly, scarcely moving our limbs? . . .

"The way to do things is neither the way of Heaven nor that of Earth but that of Man."

The way of man, according to Hsüntzu, is to learn and to work. Hard, tedious, realistic, and persistent, man's way has no room for wishful thinking, pleasant daydreaming, or effortless existence.

For centuries many of our scholars in their struggle to capture the top academic honors drew inspiration from Hsüntzu's philosophy of hard work. To him neither differences in native intelligence nor advantages in environment should bar a hard-working individual from attaining his objective. "A fast horse may be able to cover thirty feet in one gallop," he said, "but a limping one, by running incessantly, can cover many times the same distance." "What others can achieve in one attempt," he observed, "you can equal or even excel in ten."

In the sayings of Hsüntzu one can find many witty, simple, and yet wise counsels to suit every type of individual who has difficulties in realizing his ambition. For those who like to make wishes more than working for them, he said:

"The destination, however near, can never be reached unless one walks toward it. . . . The job, however easy, remains undone unless one works at it."

For those who are willing to work but unwilling to improve on their working methods, the philosopher remarked:

"For a wider vision, I would stand on the high ground rather than stretching and straining my neck at a low level. . . .

"Though your voice is not any louder, yet by yelling with the wind, it will be carried farther and heard more clearly."

Granted that a person is willing to work for his purpose in life and is willing to improve on his working methods, what will Hsüntzu advise if he gives up his pursuit in the face of seemingly unsurmountable obstacles? To the determined and persistent philosopher, no obstacle is too great to overcome. He said:

"A good farmer does not quit farming because of flood and drought. Nor will a good businessman stop trading on account of losses. . . .

"The insignificant and soft earthworms, by continuous digging, can pile the mud into a hill."

Suppose a person by working hard, by improving his working methods, and by overcoming his obstacles still fails to reap his reward in life; will not Confucian fatalism then prevail? To this, Hsüntzu explained that what is workable will work and that if it does not, something will have to be done to correct whatever has gone wrong. Comparing one's progress in life with the movement of a horse-drawn carriage, the philosopher remarked:

"Were you to have six horses to pull your carriage, you would still get nowhere should they pull it backward and forward, toward the left and the right, all at the same time."

Sensing the danger of overworking those who subscribed to his theory, he put a limit to hard work by recommending conservation of one's physical and spiritual energy. Said he:

"No matter how mighty is the river, when its sources are blocked and its banks are leveled, it will soon run empty of its water."

Developing the theme that progress is a matter of gradual accumulation of constructive human efforts and that achievement of purpose can be consummated through hard and persistent work irrespective of obstacles, Hsüntzu believed that moral perfection is within reach of everyone:

"Everybody can be a *superior man*. Pick any man on the street. If he will only learn to be good, practice it, and review his constant improvement, he too, by accumulating the good he has been achieving, will eventually arrive at the saintly goal. . . .

"Not all men have succeeded, because they never tried."

In a country where the way of the ancients stands for everything which is good and noble, any thinker who dares to differ from it risks the blame of a serious offense. Confucius, building his "ethical utopia" on the legendary reigns of our wise kings of yore, taught us to strive for the realization of our ideal past by duplicating as nearly as possible the virtuous ways of our ancestors. While most of our Confucianist thinkers joined in the chorus with the Great Sage, Hsüntzu alone dissented. Like a discordant note in an otherwise harmonious song in praise of our past, his views, in spite of their merits, sound unpleasant to Chinese ears. Believing that progress is cumulative and continuous, Hsüntzu maintained that the direction of human advancement is to proceed forward instead of going backward. Rather than to look upon the Age of Golden Rule in the past as a model to shape the present, our chief concern should be to guard ourselves from being held back by our traditions and to keep on enriching the wisdom, knowledge, and experience which we inherited from our past.

The greatest departure from orthodox Confucian thinking is Hsüntzu's contention that human nature is evil. This not only places him in direct opposition to the views of Mencius but to a certain extent to those of Confucius as well. Considering the fact that our practical thinker believes in the efficacy of human efforts, inborn goodness is by logic inadmissible to him. Whatever good there is in this world cannot be built up easily by projecting the innate goodness within us. Man must learn how to uproot his animal instincts which lead him to evil, know what is good, and cultivate it continuously and painstakingly. On that theory, it will be interesting to quote a few lines from Hsüntzu:

"Human nature is evil. . . . What is good in man is acquired. . . .

"All men more or less love money, profits, and those things which benefit them. . . . Because of it, strife is developed instead of mutual respect. . . .

"By virtue of the bestiality within us, we prefer oppressing or even killing to being loyal and faithful to one another. . . .

"Were we to leave our evil nature to itself, it will eventually lead us to strife, from strife to conflict, and from conflict to brutality. It is most important that we teach men what is good and tutor them to be good. Only then shall we enjoy mutual respect and peace."

Looking at it purely from a utilitarian point of view, Hsüntzu's theory on the evil origin of human nature seems to have taken into consideration a more realistic aspect of human problems than did the views of either Confucius or Mencius. Refuting his predecessors' contention that goodness is projected from the innate goodness within man, our philosopher feels that man cannot be expected to be good without first satisfying his more elementary instincts, and these he considers to be evil in nature. An ordinary person will not share his food with another when he himself is dying from hunger. Neither will he give his clothing and shelter to his fellow men when he is suffering from want of both. To have a heart for the other fellow is more of a sensible human creation designed for the common good than a spontaneous expression of man's innate goodness. It represents man's victory over his evil nature. Hence our sense of righteousness, moral standards, laws, government, etc., while existing for a good purpose, are not necessarily evidences of our good nature as advocated by orthodox Confucianists. "Laws, standards of righteousness, and morals are created by our wise ancestors after having studied carefully our habits and shortcomings to keep us on the right path. They are artificial and do not come from the innate goodness of human hearts," Hsüntzu concluded.

Since man's nature is evil and good things in life are artificial, what shall be our course in learning to do the good?

Differing again from the orthodox Confucianists, Hsüntzu believed that, aside from taking ethical measures such as individual character building for the attainment of an ideal human order, we must also consider the solution of conflicts of human desires which are bound to arise from human contacts. While man does not live by bread alone, bread is nevertheless as essential as spiritual nourishment. His proposal, therefore, gives equal emphasis to ethical and to materialistic problems.

On the ethical side, our aggressive thinker takes the conventional line by stressing individual character building. To him a sound character is composed of three factors— will, conduct, and thought. Will furnishes the motive power to acquire and do the good. Conduct is the channel through which the good is projected. Thought is the means by which constant improvement in character is made possible. He wrote:

"For your will power, stress training; for your conduct, stress constant improvement; and for your thought, stress progressive enlightenment. . . .

"A superior man acquires the good by fixing it firmly in his mind and absorbing it so that it becomes a part of him."

Leaving the discernment of the good to individual resources, Hsüntzu described the pursuit of the good in the following words:

"When you see that which is good, acquire it discriminatingly; and with that which is evil, warn yourself. Look up to those who correct your faults as teachers and treat those who truthfully tell you that you are right as friends. But of those who flatter you, beware!

"A superior man is never tired of the good. He listens to sound advice and corrects himself accordingly.

"A hopeless person is one who, being in the wrong, detests those who criticize him. Inconsiderate as he is, he wants others to praise him. With the heart of a tiger and the conduct of a wolf, he hates those who reprove him. He keeps away from those who correct him and takes into confidence those who flatter him. Such a person, even though he wants to be in the company of his fellow men, cannot but face eventual ruin."

For those who seek the extremes Hsüntzu prescribed the pursuit of the golden mean:

· "A superior man studies all angles of a given problem and senses the golden mean. . . .

"An obstinate temperament should be softened with tenderness. . . . Those who are courageous but fierce need understanding and patience. . . . The narrow-minded should acquire a wider outlook. . . .

"Don't let the material things possess you. Be their master."

Finally, a superior character, the product of relentless and persistent training, is acquired when a person becomes, in the words of the philosopher, increasingly "respectful and calm in his attitude, sincere and faithful in his heart, and truthful and understanding in his love for his fellow man."

More outstanding than his views on character building as a means to overcome our evil nature is Hsüntzu's proposal for adjusting conflicts of human desires arising from our daily wants. To him education and ethical instruction are not the only solutions to moral degeneration. Certain desires and wants in man must be met one way or another. Failure to do so will drive him to desperation and from desperation to the growth of unrest. The philosopher said:

"Human beings were born with certain desires. When these desires are not satisfied, they seek ways of gratification. In seeking gratification, the desires of one may conflict with those of another. This breeds disorder and disorder turns into chaos. Our ancestors sensed the root of the trouble. They created a *standard of propriety* to adjust human desires. By it, they satisfied the wants of the people with our available resources. At the same time, they regulated and developed our resources in order to keep up with the growth of human desires. Thus, by interacting on one another, wants in man and means of satisfying them advance harmoniously. . . ."

By recognizing human wants and by sensing the importance of satisfying them, Hsüntzu introduced a materialistic aspect to his philosophy which hitherto had been neglected by the orthodox Confucianists. It is significant in that moral issues, which both Confucius and Mencius considered to be ethical problems, assume a social character necessitating political and economic adjustment. Individual faults and failures alone are no longer accountable for evils in men. It is now held that evils among us increase in proportion to the degree of maladjustment between human wants and our ability to satisfy them. Conversely, the good in us, aside from being the result of moral instruction, are products of a harmonious blending of our resources with human wants. All these go back once again to Hsüntzu's central theme—that happiness can only be achieved through the way of man.

Himself a nonfatalist, Hsüntzu encountered a kind of fate to which no other philosopher in China has been subjected. His novelty in thought and aggressiveness in presentation won for him not acceptance but rejection by the bulk of our people. With the exception of a few of his sayings which our scholars have quoted every now and then as proverbs, all the principal points in his philosophy are cast aside.

Take for instance Hsüntzu's conception of human achievement. To him the life of humanity is continuous and its progress a result of gradual accumulation of man's past and present achievements. From it one might infer that our people would take his advice to heart and try to live more for the present than in the memory of the past. This, however, was not the case; for it sounded to us no more illuminating than ordinary hearsay. Did not Confucius tell us that our ancestors had long since achieved the Golden Rule? Was it not our own stupidity to have lost the virtues of our ancestors? How necessary it was for us to study our virtuous past so that by duplicating it in our time we might arrive at the supreme good as our ancestors before us arrived at theirs!

Thus for nearly twenty centuries we anchored ourselves securely on our past until our world fell under us when we were brought face to face with the new, vigorous civilization from the West. We found that our otherwise "thoroughly competent" physicians who built up their prosperous practices on the strength of the truly ancestral origin of their skills were no match for the Western doctors whose ability was based on the latest knowledge of medical science. Our manufacturers who depended on ancestral secret processes for the success and reputation of their products were cornered and driven out of their own home market by more useful but much cheaper products from the faraway West whose secret of success was its technology of the latest origin. There was a time when no pleasure was greater than to eat mutton flakes at a restaurant in Peiping roasted on an open pan which had its latest cleaning only one hundred fifty years ago. Today I wonder how many of us will still consider this famous ancient pan an outstanding feature of attraction.

It will indeed be interesting to speculate as to what would happen to China were we to follow Hsüntzu instead of Confucius. Would we be fond of the past like the British and keep on progressing as well? Or, loosing our hold on the sure-footed wisdom of Confucianism, would we not slip and fall into oblivion like many another ancient culture? As it is, we anchor on our past, neither going anywhere nor drifting aimlessly toward uncertainty.

Then there is Hsüntzu's theory about the efficacy of human efforts, or *the way of man* versus *the way of heavenly fate*, which was also more or less rejected by our people. Even though we could have thoroughly understood his point of view, still our complacent and fatalistic pattern of living was too deep-rooted and "good" to be disturbed. Life to many of us means the minimum of subsistence-seeking but the maximum of enjoyment. It would have required a good many more Hsüntzus to convince us we should enlarge on work which was considered unnecessary beyond the line of plain living and cut down on our play. And there is only one Hsüntzu among our many philosophers! However, though our aggressive thinker failed to accomplish it, our contact with the West has opened our eyes to the importance of serious work. It now remains for time to reveal where this new development will lead us.

THE TAOIST SCHOOL

VI. LAOTZU (570-460 B.C.)

CHINA'S MOST MYSTERIOUS
PHILOSOPHER

*The Taoist school of thought enables a person to con-
centrate his mind on a few things, to live without
worry, and to enjoy whatever is around him.*
—Szu-ma Ch'ien (second century B.C.)

AMONG CHINA'S PHILOSOPHERS, Confucianist or otherwise,
none can claim a more mysterious reputation or possesses
more intriguing thinking than Loatzu. As an independent
thinker he founded the Taoist school of thought. As an
atheist he subsequently became the supreme god of the
Taoist religion without his knowledge. As both, he wielded
a profound, even though not the dominant, influence
upon the way of life in China.

Confucius, reputedly the greatest mind of China, was
baffled by Laotzu. *The Book of Lün-yü* or *The Analects*,
a basic Confucian classic, has an interesting account of the
meeting of the two philosophers. Laotzu, an older man,
was already well known when Confucius, a mere young
upstart, was still roaming the four corners of China campaigning for political reforms. Always eager for self-im-

provement, Confucius went to call on Laotzu. The two met and chatted. One memorable request made by Confucius on this occasion was that he, as a younger man, might be profited by the wisdom of the venerable scholar. Whereupon Laotzu nonchalantly counseled:

"Your words will be remembered long after you are dead. But do try to rid yourself of aggressiveness and ambition. Such vanity does you not a bit of good."

After the visit Confucius returned to his disciples and told them:

"I know a bird can fly; a fish can swim; and an animal can run. But as to a dragon, I don't know what it can do! Isn't Laotzu the dragon?"

Living approximately between 570 and 460 B.C., Laotzu was about twenty years older than Confucius. In a country where earlier birth constitutes an important factor in prestige, Laotzu's seniority over Confucius has since become a favorite talking point of the Taoists. Unlike the Confucian scholars of his time who traveled up and down the country agitating for political reforms, our philosopher liked to sit down quietly in a world of his own, doing his own thinking in his own way. Laotzu's position as a librarian to the king fitted in nicely with his habit of living.

While practically all the eminent philosophers of his time were born in northern China, Laotzu came from a southern province. As southerners are considered less rigid in manners and more liberal in thoughts, he is generally regarded as the first representative of China's southern thinking.

The thoughts of Laotzu were recorded in a book entitled *Tao-te-Ching*, variably translated as *The Book of Tao* or *On the Infinite Way*. While it consists nominally of eighty chapters, there are not more than five thousand words in the whole book. No one knows how much of it was actually written by Laotzu. It is generally conceded, however, that at least the first half of the book represents correctly his philosophy. Szu-ma Ch'ien (second century B.C.), a noted authority on Chinese history, had this to say about Laotzu:

"Laotzu studied the infinite way of the Universe. He lived in the Kingdom of Chow for a long time. When that dynasty was about to fall, he left the country. At the border, the commander of the guards, who had heard of Laotzu's wisdom, demanded: 'Sir, now that you are about to depart to the yonder, will you not write a book to leave behind?' Whereupon Laotzu took time out to write The Book of Tao which consisted of five thousand words. After that he disappeared beyond the border and no one knew what became of him."

This account of Laotzu by the famous historian subsequently created one of the leading comedies in the annals of Chinese thought. By his referring mysteriously to the philosopher's knowledge of the *infinite way of the universe* and recording his miraculous disappearance beyond the border, he led our people to conclude, by putting the two accounts together, that Laotzu must have succeeded in knowing the unknowable and thereby become an immortal. Thus toward the latter part of the second century A.D. when China felt the need of a native religion to compete with the imported Buddhism, Laotzu, although an atheist, was drafted to be the presiding deity of Taoism. Here is the story.

Between the second and the first century B.C. China had rid herself of continuous civil wars and even attained a national unity. Tired as we were of the former wars, our general desire now was to relax, to do as little as possible, and to enjoy a quiet, normal, uneventful life. The philosophy of Laotzu, which concerned itself exclusively with these desires, fitted snugly the requirements of the time. Many prominent scholars developed a special fondness for his philosophy. They praised his "do-nothing-ism," the omnipotence of the infinite way of the universe, and the blending of the inner self with the rhythm of nature.

Just about this period Buddhism filtered into China from India. The alien religion, being passive in its teachings, found our people in a receptive mood. To combat the outside influence, some provincially minded patriots began to look for a native religion. But there was none in sight. True, we had Confucianism. It, however, lacked many a quality needed to satisfy the religious demand of the people. For one thing, it did not promise a glorious after life. It failed to provide either superhuman aid when we were in trouble or punishment for the bad and reward for the good. And it did not perform miracles. To rescue China from conquest by the Buddhist ideology, some kind of original teaching, preferably with a tinge of mystery, was very much wanted.

Meanwhile our scholars, driven by their overenthusiasm in the study of Laotzu, were rapidly corrupting his theories into ways of achieving immortality. Sheltering themselves under the protective wings of Taosim, they wrote books on mythical formulas, medicinal or otherwise, with the power to transform an ordinary mortal into a godly immortal. Among them was a certain Taoist practitioner by the name of Chang Dao-ling who, riding on the Taoist wave of popularity, busily engaged himself in gathering followers and selling magic formulas to the people for use against evil spirits, sickness, and every imaginable enemy of man. The philosophic Laotzu-ism, now mercilessly exploited, gradually crystallized into a popular religion with the venerable philosopher as its unwilling founder.

By the thirteenth century A.D., when the Mongols conquered China, Taoism had already grown into a full-fledged religion dispensing spiritual comforts to the masses. Kublai Khan, who was by nature a tolerant man, gave his official blessing to Taoism as he did to other religious creeds. A direct descendant of Chang Dao-ling was commissioned the spiritual ruler of the Taoist faith with headquarters at Dragon-Tiger Mountain, Kiangsi Province, China. As all Taoist priests are entitled to marry, the descendants of Chang Dao-ling, with the sanction of the subsequent emperors, succeeded in maintaining their control over the religion. During the years immediately preceding the Japanese invasion of China, "Chang, the Heavenly Priest" could be seen in his palatial monastery at that same Dragon-Tiger Mountain in Kiangsi, China. Today the Taoist priests are serving our people in much the same way as their predecessors did in time gone by. All over China, particularly in the backwoods, they are still driving away the evil spirits for our ignorant masses, curing sickness with magic formulas, rescuing the dead from hell and delivering same to heaven at a price to suit the pocket of the doubtful customers. They thrive because the bulk of our population, pending their salvation by education, are unwilling to take chances with eternity.

Leaving the religious aspects of Taoism aside, the philosophy of Laotzu is a product of the same time and environment which characterized the thoughts of Confucius, Mencius, and Hsüntzu. Ordinarily, similar cause should produce similar effect. But philosophers, being not mechanically constituted, respond differently.

From the eighth to the third century B.C. China was

more or less engulfed in wars between and among her many feudal states. To the Confucianists such a state of affairs ought to be met by ethical measures. Thus Confucius answered the challenge by propounding an ethical system to harmonize human relations. Supporting him, Mencius supplemented it with respect for the will of the people as an additional measure to curb the irresponsible activities of the rulers. Then along came Hsüntzu, who believed that the troubles were of our own making. He therefore suggested that to undo the wrongs, all of us should study our problems more seriously and solve them by persistent, laborious, minute efforts. But with Laotzu the stimulus of time and environment produced an exactly opposite effect. He felt that both the rulers and the governed were piling up their troubles by wanting to do too much. What else could have resulted from "tinkering" with this and that, he reasoned, but that we caught ourselves in a mess of human affairs of our own making! Then in our attempts to free ourselves from the entanglements, we simply kept on multiplying our difficulties. With this kind of reasoning as his background, Laotzu proposed that we rely less on our own resources, since to err was human, and taught that if we followed more the intrinsic laws of nature, all of us would not only have less to worry about but should also find ourselves in perfect harmony with Tao. Instead of fooling ourselves with man-made illusions, we all would rediscover the natural peace, poise, and happiness inherent in nature. This philosophic principle is called Tao or the *infinite way of the universe*.

In the philosophic pattern of Taoism, all matter, living or lifeless, is part of one cosmic unit. Man is just a part of the universe as are the stars, mountains, streams, trees, grasses, raindrops, and living creatures of all kinds. Despite our ability to think and act, we can no more exist independently of the laws of nature than can other forms of creation. While the universe functions smoothly and harmoniously in the endless span of time and space, man, a tiny particle in the vast creation, encounters almost continual wars and troubles. This is because the way of nature harmonizes with the principles of Tao, whereas man relies on his insignificant mortal faculties for guidance.

There are many passages in Laotzu's book which describe Tao. Some are either too deep to be understood or too mysterious to be studied. In one chapter, for instance, Tao is described as that which cannot be seen, heard, and felt; it has neither substance nor form; it is timeless and spaceless. For our present purpose we will have to depend on the plainer part of The Book of Tao for a definition. The following quotation will be of value:

"Tao is beginningless and endless. To its being, all forms of matter, living and lifeless, owe their existence. —I don't know what to call it. Arbitrarily, I name it Tao."

From the foregoing passage many scholars of Taoism conclude that since the grand principle of Tao is the ultimate explanation of creation, then by acquainting ourselves with its qualities and by adapting our way of life in conformity thereto, we should be able to discover the true wisdom of living. Unfortunately Laotzu, while proposing that the way of Tao take the place of the way of man, was uncertain as to its true nature. He said so a number of times in his book. However, by piecing together his various observations it may be said that Tao, the mysterious principle of the universe, reveals itself through four phases of expression. These are its normalcy, naturalness, selflessness, and nothingness.

Normalcy is the antithesis of that which is artificial,

abnormal, uncommon, extraordinary. Were the universe to reverse its normal rhythm, it would cease to function. For the sun to rise from the west and set in the east would indeed be an unusual attraction. But nature never tried it, because it is contrary to *Tao*. Man somehow knows this too. He neither expects spring to follow summer nor autumn to follow winter. He also knows that rice which is to be planted in spring cannot grow if it is planted in winter. In fact, man knows so much about the ordinary ways of nature that when it comes to human affairs, he forgets that the same principle applies.

Contrary to *Tao*, man acts where nature avoids. Himself an undetachable element in nature's vast pattern of things, he persists in getting away from its invisible but all-embracing rules. Instead of regarding normalcy as the most stable influence in the world, he prizes the exceptional, the unusual, and the uncommon.

Among man's artificial possessions, Laotzu singles out our conceptions of beauty and virtue as contrary to *Tao*. As man-made qualities, beauty and virtue are cherished because they are rare, exceptional, and have a wholesome influence on the ugly and the unvirtuous. This fact, comforting to most of us, is obnoxious, deplorable, and un-*Tao*-ly to the venerable philosopher. Instead of seeing here a progressive sign, Laotzu regards the very presence of these values a proof of pathological characteristics in human society. Unless there is an abundance of ugliness and evil, why should beauty and virtue be so highly esteemed? The higher we evaluate beauty and virtue, the more must we admit our increasing ugliness and evil. These abnormal contrasts are artificial standards made by man to divide humanity into two camps—the virtuous few and the evil majority. As long as they exist, men can never hope to live in harmony with one another. To unite with Tao, commonness and normalcy must prevail in human relations as they do in the invisible rhythm of nature. Wrote Laotzu:

"When the world knows what is beautiful, then ugliness must exist. When it knows what is good, then there must be evil too. . . .

"The virtuous and the courageous are esteemed when the true way of life disappears. For then the wise are discovered in the presence of hypocrisy; filial piety is valued to curb disharmony in the family; and faithful public servants are respected in view of the chaos in the country. . . .

"Therefore when the sage acts, he does nothing; when he speaks, he is silent. . . .

"Tao does nothing and everything is done by virtue of it. . . ."

We cannot say that Laotzu's observations on normalcy are unsound. But it must be admitted that their actual application is difficult. How are we to discourage the ugly and the evil among us if we do not stand up for beauty and virtue? How are we to attain eventual perfection if we do not continually search for it? What will happen to society if we are to abolish our sense of justice, our moral standards, and other "artificial institutions" such as laws and government designed for social control? Curiously enough, the Taoist scholars after Laotzu, by exercising their sense of balance and not discounting Confucianist influences on them, chose to deviate from his purely "nihilistic" and "anarchistic" thoughts. They maintained that Laotzu did not intend to abolish our existing moral institutions first and then institute normalcy. To the contrary, the venerable philosopher merely wanted to point out the effectiveness of 潛移默化, the power to influence and convert people by gradual, invisible, and silent ways. In other words, we are to follow goodness and virtue as our standards of conduct but not to regard them as something rare, precious, superior, or to be esteemed. Instead of shouting loudly for the good things in life, we should silently practice the good and the virtuous ways as a matter of course. Rather than as a subject matter to be taught or exhibited, it should be regarded simply as an ordinary way of life to which all the people are to be unconsciously drawn and assimilated. That is exactly what Laotzu meant, so they explained, when he said: "When the sage acts, he does nothing; when he teaches, he is silent. . . . Tao does nothing and everything is done by virtue of it."

Another quality of Tao is its naturalness. This idea springs from a general observation about which we can hardly find fault. Stars are stars because they are naturally so. Plants sprout, take roots, grow, reproduce, age, and finally die. This, too, is naturally so. In fact, all matter, living or lifeless, came into being through a natural process. There can be no other way.

As a particle in the pattern of universe, a man shares with other forms of matter the same quality of naturalness. Being neither good nor evil, neither personal nor impersonal, neither spiritual nor materialistic, is simply naturally so with us. To find similarities between man's naturalness and that of the natural phenomena around us is already difficult enough. How much more so when we have to transfer our findings, vague and intangible and obscure as they must be, into our way of living! This, however, nothing less, is what the Taoists propose to do.

Laotzu's solution to the problem is as unusual and unorthodox as are his views on other aspects of Tao. Direct and simple, he remarked: "Be like the infants!" It seems that babies, having neither the faculty of appreciating our artificial ways of life nor the opportunity of acquiring them, possess more tincture of *Tao* than the grownups. Therefore if we are to find out about the natural pattern of living, the behavior of babies ought to be a good starting point.

True to the conventional form of Chinese philosophic writings, which consisted mostly of straight assertions without further elaboration or proof, Laotzu failed to mention just what are the ways of the infants. This means that the students studying his philosophy must rely on their own resources to make the correct guesses. Incidentally it is the interpretations by the readers of the brief sayings of the philosophers which make the study of Chinese philosophy interesting.

This paragraph, which deals with the behavior of the infants, represents the personal interpretation of Laotzu by the writer. Neither scientific nor pragmatic, it is inserted here merely as an illustration of how some of us study our ancient philosophy. Unlike grownups, infants possess a marked degree of poise and relaxation when they sleep, eat, and do the things they generally do while awake. Instead of counting the sheep to induce sleep or tossing here and there wondering why it is difficult to go to sleep, babies take it as a matter of course until we encourage them to "fuss." In fact, many of us will be appalled when we compare the sweet composure of a sleeping baby with the distorted and sometimes horrible expression on a dozing grownup. Babies enjoy simple food and loathe the taste and smell of certain mixtures which grownups consider to be indispensable to "fashionable living." They object to over-greased and -seasoned foods as much as we like to indulge in them. A baby has more sense in not smoking than a grownup in wanting to part with it. Watch the natural posture of a normal and healthy baby and many a round-shouldered and chest-depressed grownup ought to be ashamed! Furthermore, infants' interest in life is enormous. Practically everything arouses their enthusiasm and amuses them accordingly. They smile, they jump, and they are happy because their sense of humor is simple, innocent, and devoid of sharpness and complicated feelings. But more wonderful still, babies have a universal outlook on life. They consider animals, insects, grass, flowers, pebbles, or any objects, living or lifeless, as their equals. They do not hesitate to enter into conversation, to wave "bye-bye," or even to indulge in more intimate gestures with any of these objects. In fact they are so advanced in their cosmic view of life that beside it even the most advanced type of grownup liberalism stands no comparison. Yes, all of us, at one time or another, were babies and possessed "sweet, unspoiled, innocent, and truthful natures." The years might have added some ugly things or subtracted some beautiful things from us. When Laotzu observed that babyhood reflected the way of nature, did he really mean that we should stop spoiling further our original babyish qualities and try to be simple, trusting, and natural once more? I somehow think he did. Said he in his book: "Hold on to the unique qualities of your nature and never depart from them."

Selflessness, according to Laotzu, is another quality of Tao which should be a standard for our natural way of life. It seems that the universe, which has been in existence beyond the scope of time and space, is never conscious of its own being. Because it is interested neither in the rotation of heavenly bodies nor in the cycles of life on earth, its influence has been felt everywhere. Were Tao, the supreme principle of the universe, interested in one thing or another, the whole cosmic system would have long ago ceased to function. Wrote Laotzu:

"Heaven and earth, perpetual as they are, do not interest themselves in their own preservation. Yet, by virtue of them, all matter, living and lifeless, have their existence. Likewise, a wise man is he who, having forgotten his own person, obtains thereby the true life."

Most of our troubles and much of our unhappiness come from our reluctance to part with self-interest. Take worry for example. Some of us worry "defensively" for fear that something may happen to our person or property if we do not watch out. Others worry "aggressively," who, having had enough or more than enough to live on, torture themselves by devising ways and means to acquire some more from someone else. These things, which are going on all the time, constitute the bulk of our problems. And the root is selfishness.

Our problems will disappear, contended Laotzu, if we follow the way of Tao by pulling ourselves out of the circle of self-interest. He remarked:

"When sudden luck or misfortune comes to a person, he regards it with alarm. He worries about what is going to happen to him. All these are due to his inability to forget himself. When he shall have succeeded in detaching himself from the consideration of his interest, what else can further trouble him?"

There is also a tactical angle to selfless living. A self-conscious person is not natural. He has great difficulties in handling himself, not to mention handling those with whom he associates. Equally unnatural is a self-centered person who denies others the right to the same consideration as himself. Man is like a frog at the bottom of the well: all that it knows about heaven is the tiny speck of celestial space which it sees. Selfless living, founded on the principle of Tao, is like a self-illuminating star which shines through its own worthiness. Explained Laotzu:

"A truly understandable person does not have to explain for himself; a truly illustrious person does not have to publicize his fame; and a truly respected person does not have to praise himself.

"If a man makes no issue with himself, no one cares to make an issue with him."

Finally, nothingness, as a quality of Tao, is considered the outstanding characteristic of Laotzu's philosophy. Whenever a Taoist scholar is asked to describe Tao, the first thing which enters his mind is the philosopher's remark, "Tao does nothing, and everything is done by virtue of it."

It is absurd to assume that anything can be accomplished without working for it. Some of our witty scholars seem to think that this phase of Laotzu's philosophy is accountable for China's irresponsible, happy-go-lucky, romantic pattern of living. Others, sensing the prevalence of confusion and hopelessness in those days, have interpreted nothingness as the philosopher's reaction to his time and circumstances. Since nothing is worth while in this world, why should a man labor, sweat, and worry till the end of his mortal days? Explanations such as these cannot be dismissed lightly, for they do penetrate into our ways of living. A familiar proverb often quoted by the Chinese reads: "The world would have been quiet and peaceful were it not for the fools who constantly make a mess of it." Uninterested in and detached from human turmoil, many of us in China did manage to enjoy "do-nothing-ism" and de-

rive an almost unearthly pleasure from being able to see
things through. But are these views really intended by
Laotzu?

A careful study of Laotzu's "do-nothing-ism" reveals
that it is not as superficial as some of our scholars have
interpreted it to be. While it is true that when the philosopher first propounded the doctrine, he wanted the rulers
of his time, who were piling up troubles for everybody by
wanting to do too much, to make themselves useful by
observing "do-nothing-ism," it must be stressed also—and
more importantly, too—that beneath this simple advice
lies a series of deep philosophical observations.

Instead of being the cause of an effect, "do-nothing-ism"
is the effect of a cause. As the principle of the universe,
Tao guides the cosmic system so rhythmically and automatically that it functions as if no effort is required. Applying this to man's way of life, a true "do-nothing-ist" is
one who, having learned the essence of Tao, conducts his
life with such skill and finesse that he glides through life
without exertion and mishaps.

That this is an important phase in the art of living
seems to be demonstrated in many of our daily activities.
Laotzu observed:

"He who walks skillfully leaves no tracks behind. He
who speaks well leaves no ground for argument. He who
figures well requires no help from the counting sticks."
Here the effortless and relaxed manner in which a truly
expert hiker, speaker, or accountant displayed his specialty
is used by the philosopher to demonstrate the inner meaning of "do-nothing-ism." In our modern life, we too observe the advantages which a calm and steady person
usually enjoys over his tense and nervous competitor, be
it in the field of athletics or business pursuits. As a way of

life, it embodies the essence of poise, confidence, wisdom. Just as the universe, working rhythmically and automatically, appears to man as an effortless phenomenon, so must man assimilate its true essence in his application of Tao.

"Do-nothing-ism," being modeled after the way of nature, is said to possess a quality which is weak without but strong within. Or, as Laotzu would say it: "Be possessed of the strength of the male but display the weakness of the female." Accentuating the quality of weakness, the philosopher saw in the behavior of water a pattern for his Taoist way of life. Commenting on its intrinsic wisdom, he observed: "Water nourishes all things but fights not." It seems to him that on the surface, water, being soft, passive and fluid, is female in quality. But when one takes notice of how it flows down from the mountains, forms the mighty river, cuts through rocks and barriers unconsciously, effortlessly, and naturally, and nourishes the valley where it passes, its strength is decidedly male. It is therefore akin to Tao because, hiding its "strength of the male" and displaying its "weakness of the female," it accomplishes the purposes for which it is designed. Applying the same principles to the way of man, a Taoist will be the one who understands the true contours of human topography and who is able to conduct himself in such a manner that he not only glides through life as effortlessly and constructively as the flow of water but in addition enriches the fields of humanity in the same way the water the valley.

A discourse on Taoism will not be complete unless it includes Laotzu's theory of governmentless government. Just as do-nothing-ism is to be the guide of the individual way of life, so shall it be for the conduct of government.

Because the politicians seem to be wanting to do things all the time, the philosopher has little faith in them. A silkworm, for instance, might have saved its own life if it had adhered to "do-nothing-ism." But wanting to do things all the time, it spins a silken cocoon to imprison itself in and eventually seals its own fate. Similarly, government problems will continue to increase as long as those who run the country keep on "tinkering" with human affairs. Wrote Laotzu:

"People are hard to govern because those who rule do too many things. . . .

"People are hungry because there are too many persons living on taxes. Lawbreakers increase as more statutes are put into effect. . . .

"I do nothing, naturally the people will have to manage their own affairs; I am fond of quietude, naturally the people will reform themselves; I handle no business, naturally the people will be rich themselves; I entertain no desires, naturally the people will be plain and honest by themselves. . . ."

Should "do-nothing-ism" prevail in politics, Laotzu believed, then an ideal society blessed by the absence of artificial boundaries and man-made racial consciousness will eventually come into being. It will consist of a number of self-sufficient communities living simply among themselves, each unit minding its own business. Mankind, by virtue of abiding with *Tao*, will then live happily. Laotzu said:

"Let the people eat well, beautify their clothing, live comfortably in their homes and enjoy their respective customs. . . .

"Settled in separate communities virtually overlooking one another, the people can hear their dogs barking and cocks crowing, but till the end of their days each unit will have nothing to do with the other."

By stripping life of its unnecessary complications, burdens, and troubles and by viewing life in its simplest and plainest form, Taoism has sought to establish a way of life which is to be satisfying, understanding, peaceful, and wise. Although we have not taken up its doctrines as completely as we did those of Confucianism, many of our eminent scholars in following the Taoist ways have been able to enjoy life in the face of disappointment, privation, and uncertainty. It is living in its original and natural form that the Taoists recommend. For the cumbersome "trimmings" created by man more often than not trouble us instead of helping us.

Szu-ma Ch'ien, a great historian of the second century B.C., after reviewing Taoist thought, appropriately remarked:

"The Taoist school of thought enables a person to concentrate his mind on a few things, to live without worry, and to enjoy whatever is around him. . . .

"The Taoists handle human affairs by following the trend of time and events. It is simple and easy to master. It accomplishes more with less effort."

MOTZU'S SCHOOL OF THOUGHT

VII. MOTZU (Approximately 468–390 B.C.)

EXPONENT OF UNIVERSAL LOVE

> *Motzu and his followers harm not the weak, rescue people from fights, abhor aggression, advocate disarmament and labor to save the world.*
>
> —Chuang-tzu (third century B.C.)

THE PHILOSOPHIC FATE of Motzu is as strange as that of Laotzu. The latter, in spite of his atheistic thought, subsequently became the "supreme god" of the Taoist religion. And to this day those who worship him as a god still outnumber many times those who study him as a philosopher. But Motzu, who was really the founder of a religious sect, the exponent of religious ideals, and the rescuer from human miseries, only succeeded in impressing our people as a thinker. No amount of explanation will clear up the paradoxical positions occupied by the two philosophers in respect to their thoughts. It simply happens to be so.

The exact dates of Motzu's birth and death are uncertain and have been variably estimated by our scholars. The period of 468–390 B.C. shown in the chapter heading, although merely approximate, is probably not far wrong.

Living at a time when China was continuously in the

grip of feudal wars, Motzu believed that all our troubles could be solved if our people would only learn to love one another, to be thrifty, and to fear the retributive power of Heaven. Instead of campaigning for political reforms such as were undertaken by the Confucianists or of advocating "do-nothing-ism" as was the case with the Taoists, the philosopher felt that the most effective way to right the wrongs was to take practical measures himself whenever and wherever possible. To this end he organized his followers into a strictly disciplined religious order, forsaking all earthly rewards and pleasures, and preached and practiced three principal doctrines: to love one another as a cure of constant wars, to conserve materials as a remedy for poverty, and to understand the will of Heaven as a guide to conduct.

From his contemporaries Motzu attracted considerable attention by his "do-it" spirit. Chuang-tzu, a noted Taoist philosopher of the third century B.C., wrote: "Motzu and his followers wore coarse clothing and worked untiringly day and night for the welfare of others. They never harmed the weak. They rescued people from the ravages of war. They advocated disarmament and abolishment of aggression. They labored to save the world." Mencius, third century B.C., second in prominence only to Confucius, said in his book: "Motzu would do anything to benefit the people even if it brought him great personal sufferings." Hsüntzu, another outstanding Confucian thinker of the third century B.C., commented: "Motzu would not stop doing things for the welfare of the world till he was utterly exhausted."

While many a contemporary thinker wrote highly of the philosopher, Motzu himself was very particular in evaluating the teachings of the rival schools, especially those of the Confucianists. To him Confucian pragmatism is not inclusive enough to satisfy his desire for knowledge. Besides the *what*, he also wants to inquire into the *why* and the *how*.

One day a group of Confucianists was discussing "How to Be a Good Administrator," and Motzu happened to be listening in. All that was said revolved around a familiar quotation from Confucius describing a good administrator as "one who is well liked by those near him and who attracts support from those away from him." Apparently the Confucian way of thinking was to restrict their theme to an analytical study of a given term and to leave the *why* and *how* to be worked out independently by the individual. Irritated and dissatisfied with their narrow scope of thought, Motzu retorted: "What is more important is why a good administrator is well liked and supported and how he achieves it!"

This casual criticism of the Confucianists earned for Motzu an unusual position in the history of Chinese thought. Being the first one to stress the importance of presenting one's theme logically and systematically, he was credited with introducing the logical method of thinking to Chinese philosophy. In holding to be insufficient the loosely correlated sayings and observations which distinguished the Confucianist and Taoist writings of his day, Motzu probably was the first philosopher to initiate organized thinking. He wrote:

"Speak with a logical pattern. Can your theme be substantiated by the facts of the past? Is it practical, useful, and wanted by the people? After being put into practice, will your theme actually bring about the anticipated benefits to the people and the country?"

From these words one gets a fairly clear picture of the

basis of Motzu's philosophical outlook. To him one's life should be dedicated to serving the people and the country through a realistic approach and practical deeds. Thus instead of confining himself strictly to philosophic contemplation, Motzu devoted a good part of his life to putting into practice what he believed to be right. A thinker and a doer, it is a pity that our people should have overlooked many of his valuable teachings.

Convinced that human problems and troubles are created by the selfish and nearsighted activities of the individual or groups of individuals, Motzu felt that the only cure lies in the acquisition of an all-embracing love as the standard of conduct in men's dealings with one another. He wrote:

"Disorders arise from lack of mutual love among men. A thief loves what is his and cares not what belongs to others. Consequently he steals from others to enrich himself. . . .

"If the peoples of the world will only love one another as they love themselves, nations will no longer attack one another; families will no longer harm one another; and individuals will no longer rob one another. . . .

"Peace prevails when men practice mutual love and mutual help. Troubles result when men dislike each other's differences and commence to do harm to one another. . . .

"To die fighting for one's country is a hard thing to do. Yet man will do it when properly led and encouraged. Then why can't we love one another, knowing that doing so is to our mutual benefit?"

In search of a theocratic basis for his theory, Motzu propounded further the doctrine that the will of Heaven is omnipotent and omnipresent; that man must of necessity obey the will of Heaven; that *universal love and mutual* assistance is the expressed wish of Heaven; and that therefore men must love and help one another in order to prosper and progress. In the following words he stated his case:

"My conception of heavenly will can be compared to the ruler used by the carpenter. That which fits the measurement is correct, otherwise wrong. . . .

"At present, many books have been written and many words spoken on the subject of virtue. But they are far from being right. I know it is so by measuring these ideals with the will of Heaven. . . .

"Heaven decrees that men shall love and help one another. I know it is so because the wise emperors before us were blessed with happiness and prosperity by following this sacred decree. . . . Whereas those who continued to dislike and harm one another were invariably punished by the consequences. . . .

"Heaven loves the people of the world because it provides them with things to live on and to be benefited from. . . . It wants people to love one another as It loves them. . . . Otherwise why should calamities fall upon those who kill one another?"

As far as Motzu's arguments are concerned, there is very little ground left for us either to criticize him or refute him. After all, if mutual love and assistance is not the expressed will of Heaven, then why is it that in human experiences prosperity and happiness come to those who love and help one another, while war, chaos, and misery visit those who hate and destroy one another? Is there not revealed from the lessons of life a solemn principle that, whether it is the will of Heaven to the Chinese or the divine will to the Christians, the All Highest wants us to love and help one another? No wonder Motzu stands aghast at the unwillingness and the inability of mankind to understand such a simple principle as he has observed. It is indeed ironic to him, and possibly to many who subscribe to his views, that humanity will rather persist in hatred, prejudice, selfishness, and greed, and to suffer the evil consequences therefrom, than to build happiness, peace, and harmony through mutual love and the spirit of helpfulness.

From his deep conviction in the efficacy of love and mutual helpfulness as the solution to human problems, Motzu developed a strong antagonism toward the ravaging wars that were being waged by the feudal lords of his day. As a practical pacifist he not only voiced his opposition to wars of all kinds but with the support of his followers did what he could to restore peace.

In his essays against aggression, written more than two thousand years ago, the philosopher condemned war with the following words:

"We now have a man, who, after forcing himself into somebody's farm, steals the latter's peaches and plums. Those who hear about the theft will unhesitatingly say that the man is wrong. The officers who catch him will certainly punish him, because he has harmed others to benefit himself.

"Now let us suppose that the same man steals horses and cattle instead of peaches and plums. His wrong will be more serious and consequently his punishment will be more severe. As he harms others more, so shall his act of criminality increase.

"Now let us suppose further that the same man commits a murder. The seriousness of his wrong and the punishment to be meted him will increase correspondingly with the degree of harm he has done to others for the benefit of himself. . . .

"At this very moment, nations are committing far bigger wrongs by attacking one another. People not only fail to condemn them but actually praise them. Can it be said that men have yet learned to differentiate the right from the wrong? Knowing that to kill ten persons is ten times as serious as to kill one, why then does our sense fail us when it comes to large-scale slaughtering in wars? . . .

"This is exactly what I have in mind when I say that the root of the present disorders is our inability to differentiate the right from the wrong."

After reasoning out how unjustifiable and wrong it was to resort to war, Motzu went on to say in the same essay that in initiating warfare, people's livelihood would be upset; that the required armament meant waste of materials which could otherwise be used for gainful purposes; and that the sacrifices in lives due to hunger, disease, and combat could never be repaid by the spoils of war.

Illustrating the importance of unity of belief and action, *The Book of Motzu* gives an account of how the philosopher and his followers succeeded in stopping an aggressive attack of a warring king on his weaker neighbor.

It so happened that in one of the warring states a clever craftsman invented a new offensive weapon to be used in scaling the city walls, which at that time constituted the main bulwark of defense of the weak against the strong. Being a loyal subject, the inventor presented the weapon to his king. After several successful trials His Majesty was so impressed with its effectiveness that he decided to use it to conquer a neighboring state.

Somehow the bad news reached Motzu. Anxious to spare the people from the sufferings of war, and knowing that the warring king was beyond the influence of ethical considerations, Motzu sent three hundred disciples from his organization to help defend the intended victim, while he himself rushed to see the aggressive king. In making the hurried trip, the philosopher journeyed ten days and nights without stop, arriving with his clothes tattered and soles bleeding.

Impressing the king with the importance of testing out once more the effectiveness of the new weapon, Motzu persuaded His Majesty to summon the inventor to engage in a contest of offensive and defensive technique. In the ensuing match the new weapon was used in nine successive attacks against Motzu's defenses, and each time it was skillfully repelled by the pacifist philosopher.

The success of Motzu dismayed the king. Turning to the inventor for advice, the king asked: "What shall we do now?"

"Sire," counseled the loser, "we can kill Motzu. With him out of the way," he continued, "there will be no obstacle blocking us."

Smiling at the king, the pacifist philosopher said: "Your Majesty, killing me can hardly help you now. I have already sent disciples to your neighbor to aid them with my method of defense."

Finding the new weapon useless, the king dropped his proposed war.

As a realistic thinker combining convictions with corresponding actions, Motzu further proposed that in order to render service effectively one must adhere to self-denial as the way of life. Unlike the Confucianists, who appraised ideals mainly on the basis of moral values, our philosopher judged their usefulness from the beneficial effects to be derived from practical applications. Instead of talking, arguing, and dreaming over what is humanity's ultimate goal and what virtue or virtues will lead us there, Motzu-ism is committed to transforming ideals into realities. To qualify for the role, one must practice self-denial and like it.

Effective service requires concentration of mind and singleness of purpose. By denying oneself the ordinary comforts of life and by reducing living to its simplest form, Motzu believed that a person will be in a better position to devote his whole being to the service of humanity than were he to indulge in the softening influences of ease. Thus, throughout his life our philosopher not only practiced self-denial himself but was equally insistent on it for those who joined his cause. Believing that luxurious but appendix-like "trimmings" of life deprived people of their time and energy to pursue the more useful virtues of mutual love and helpfulness, Motzu carried his doctrine so far that he even demanded of the people as a whole that they give up music, good food, spacious accommodations, and cumbersome social customs in favor of simpleness and plainness. Utilitarian in outlook and "puritanic" in substance, he apparently believed that a camel overburdened with luxurious commodities will have neither energy nor "loading space" to spare for a useful load. Therefore, lest complicated and luxurious living crowd out a simple, plain, virtuous, and useful career, he made self-denial as much a part of Motzu-ism as the love and mutual helpfulness which it preaches.

Among the articles of faith which he so zealously championed, Motzu's insistence on "universalization of moral standards" might be considered his greatest contribution to Chinese humanism. It appeared to him that, although men knew how much good could come from loving and helping one another, they rather chose to face the consequences of prejudice and hatred than to enlarge the scope of its application beyond their immediate circles. If any sense of *universality* exists amongst us, it is narrowly confined to our concern for the well-being of ourselves, of our family, and perhaps of our fellow countrymen. As to the welfare of those not of our kind or nationality, whatever we do for them is incidental. Yes, universal love has failed to materialize because men preferred *differentiation* to *universalization*. Not only did we pay more attention to differences among us than to our essential oneness, but by stressing how differently some of us lived, looked, and believed, we kept mankind further and further apart from one another. Therefore, according to Motzu, we should, in addition to dropping those barriers which have separated us, develop those similarities among us which will help us unite into one world.

Another aspect of universalization is the application of our moral concepts on a universal basis. As a realistic thinker Motzu seemed to favor measuring our understanding of a given virtue from how faithfully we have put it into practice on a world-wide scale. To him, though a person might have learned the meaning of justice, what good could it do if in actual application he only insisted that justice be dealt to him and not from him? The members of a family might have mastered the intricate art of living harmoniously, happily, and affectionately together. But what good could it do if as a unit it was engaged in breaking up or otherwise interfering with the harmony and happiness of other families? On the same logic, a state may have succeeded in making the principles of righteousness, justice, equality, fraternity, orderliness prevail within its own borders. But again, what good can it do if in its dealings with other states or peoples it is entirely unmindful of their welfare and problems or even bent on ruthless exploitation? The meaning we attached to our moral concepts might be the same, but we could not be considered true to ourselves if we applied them on a differential basis to different groups of our fellow men. "Heaven decrees that men shall love and help one another," commented Motzu. And we can only be in oneness with the will of Heaven when we apply our moral concepts to our fellow beings universally and without distinction, discrimination, or differentiation.

Not all of Motzu's philosophy is as sound as what I have related thus far. Dominated by his utilitarian considerations, the philosopher did not hesitate to affirm a current belief among the Chinese of his time that there were spirits everywhere and in every object who watched our deeds vigilantly and continuously. Believing them capable of punishing us for our evil conduct as well as rewarding us for our good deeds, Motzu taught our people to fear the spirits and mind our behavior accordingly. Rather than to prove the existence of ghosts as I would like him to do, his writings only stress the usefulness of the fear of the spirits as a coercive measure to make the people behave. The intellectual weakness thus displayed by Motzu contributed in no small degree toward a subsequent cool reception of his theories by our scholars. Furthermore, accustomed to space our living at an even tempo and unwilling to sacrific the present for some indefinite happiness of the future, our people as a whole found it difficult to subscribe fully to his philosophy of self-denial and self-sacrifice. To love one another and to be helpful to one another is a good doctrine, but to get people to sacrifice everything to make it work is too hard an assignment even for the altruistic, zealous, and visionary Motzu.

THE BUREAUCRATIC SCHOOL

VIII. KUAN-CHUNG AND HIS PHILOSO-
PHY OF BUREAUCRACY

Kuan-chung handles matters relating to public admin-
istration with prudence; favors promotion of trade and
exchange of goods; wants the obligation to work dis-
tributed equitably among his people; and does every-
thing to develop natural resources. By teaching his
people the tenets of propriety, moral courage, purity,
and honor, he improves their way of life.
—Ch'ao Kuang-wu (twelfth century A.D.)

WHILE MOST of China's philosophers devote their thoughts
to virtuous living exclusively, there are a few among them
who think in terms of food, clothing, and shelter. They
more or less put an accent on earthly things and believe
that the crest of human achievement—which to them is
synonymous with prosperity, orderliness, and harmonious
living—can be achieved by way of law. These "hard-boiled"
philosophers are classified by our scholars as Fa-chia, meaning literally law-family, or more specifically, the proponents of *government by law.*

Kuan-chung, of seventh century B.C. legend, was by far
the most typical thinker of this school. Believing that
everything or practically everything can be accomplished
through legislative channels, he advocated regulation of

the lives of the people by professional rulers, promotion of the economic well-being of the people by legislation, and even enforcement of an ethical code of conduct by legal measures. If another name is needed to identify his theories, I am perfectly willing to call it the philosophy of bureaucracy. To Kuan-chung, the officeholder had the right to control the public and personal affairs of the individual.

In presenting Kuan-chung's philosophy there is a little discrepancy in dates which must be clarified. As a historical character, Kuan-chung is known to the Chinese as prime minister to the Duke of Ch'i in the seventh century B.C. But *The Book of Kuan-chung*, from which we learn of his philosophy, was written by a ghost writer sometime in the fourth to the third century B.C.

The practice of writing a book in the name of an ancient celebrity is not uncommon in China. In a land where priority in birth implies prestige and respect, a young upstart has a better chance to be heard by presenting his views in the garb of an ancient person than by using his own name. So when I refer to the thoughts of Kuan-chung in this chapter, please bear in mind that it is the anonymous writer, probably a contemporary of the early Confucianist thinkers, that I am actually talking about.

Kuan-chung, being of seventh-century B.C. vintage, naturally provided much inspiration for our anonymous writer. As an able administrator he was instrumental in making Ch'i the wealthiest and strongest state in China. By virtue of this accomplishment, the alien hordes to the north of Ch'i were unable to cross its border to attack weaker states beyond. Commenting on the legend, even Confucius exclaimed: "Were it not for Kuan-chung, we would have been in the garb of barbarians!" Our unknown author probably believed in the authenticity of the legend.

Fascinated by Kuan-chung's accomplishments and ability in public administration, he made a thorough study of the philosopher's life and went ahead writing *The Book of Kuan-chung*. It was unthinkable that a celebrated character such as Kuan-chung had no book to leave behind for posterity!

While Confucianists and other moralistic philosophers considered materialistic enrichment of life a small matter of no importance, Kuan-chung made it the mainstay of his thoughts. If there was anything which irritated our proponents of virtuous living, it was to shift our concern from moral conduct to food, clothing, and profits. No wonder that when Mencius was asked to comment on Kuan-chung, he coldly remarked: "Oh! Him? I would be ashamed to be in his company!"

Rather than protect himself under a moralistic garb, Kuan-chung was ready to admit his own shortcomings. Szu-ma Ch'ien, a noted historian of the second century B.C., recounted a story told by the philosopher:

"I and my partner Pao-shu once did business together. In dividing the profits, I always took more than my share. Pao-shu never thought that I was greedy. He knew I was poor. Once I tried to get an official position for him and failed. Pao-shu did not think that I was a fool. He knew that the chances of success were against me. When subsequently I went into government work myself, I was dismissed by my king three times in succession. Pao-shu did not think that I had no ability. He knew my time had not come. I was also in war three times. Each time I ran away. He did not consider me a coward. He knew I was worried about my aged mother. . . ."

At a time when the pursuit of virtuous living was practically the only subject worthy of discussion by China's thinkers, it needed a man of Kuan-chung's caliber who was unafraid to acknowledge his own shortcomings to propose that fostering our economic well-being in this life should be our chief concern. This attitude probably disturbed a number of moralistic scholars at the time. Even a generous soul like Confucius, when asked to comment on Kuan-chung, could only say: "He was good in his own way."

In formulating his economic theory Kuan-chung was not as anxious to give our people some degree of happiness by stepping up their productive capacity as to use it as a weapon for strengthening the power of the state. At no time did he ever speak of economic development as apart from the state. I quote:

"Among the objectives of government, to enrich the people is of first importance. . . ."

"On the deficit or surplus of the people's wealth depends the decline or rise of a nation. . . ."

"When the people have no property of their own to care for, the nation is in danger. . . ."

"When the government spends lavishly, public expenses go up. This breeds poverty. Poverty breeds crookedness. Crookedness leads to wrongdoing. And crimes are the results of economic deficiency. . . ."

"People will mind virtues when their granaries are full. They will develop a sense of honor when there is enough food and clothing."

These statements and many others point to Kuan-chung's contention that economic soundness is of primary importance to national well-being, that it is the duty of men in public office to undertake the matter for the people, and that the object of economic development is to strengthen the power of the state.

It never occurred to Kuan-chung that to educate the people to care for their own affairs would be an easier way than to have the government doing it for them. Believing that the people were too helpless to do things for themselves, he insisted that all good things should be done for them by the government. And from this thought comes the philosopher's recommendation that *government by law* is the best way to bring about a strong, orderly, and wealthy nation. He declared:

"The wise man can make laws, but without laws he cannot govern the nation. It is like a crafty workman who can make ruler and compass but without them can hardly draw perfect squares and circles. . . ."

"Law is the right way under Heaven by which saintly rulers abide. . . ."

"A saintly ruler relies on laws and not on his own intelligence."

Since law was the one and only instrument of government, the rulers who had laws in their hands counted heavily in Kuan-chung's scheme of things. On them fell the burden of doing good things as well as eradicating bad things for the people. He said:

"To be right and proper, people must be ruled. They will be satisfied when they are given security. . . ."

"Control by regulations is the best way to secure orderliness. But if the people are controlled too tightly, they will be desperate. Desperation will cause them to lose their sense of balance. On the other hand, if the control is too loose, they will do what they want. With too much freedom, selfishness will possess them and public well-being will be endangered. It is most important for the ruler to determine the degree of control required."

Although the people had little to do with actual management of national affairs, it did not mean that the rulers could do as they pleased. They too should submit to the rule by law. In fact, to assure bureaucratic efficiency Kuan-chung recommended:

"Execute those who failed to carry out an order in full, or those who carried out an order into excess, or those who failed to act on an order, or those who delayed the execution of an order, or those who disobeyed an order." It is a good thing that the Chinese are not impressed by Kuan-chung's views. For on the subject of executing incompetent government workers alone, the consequences could be very serious.

Since the people, as a body, are the tool of the state, it follows logically that in addition to being regimented into various productive activities, they should also be welded into one solid spiritual entity through uniform moralistic teachings. To this effect he remarked:

"Propriety, moral courage, purity, and the sense of honor are the four pillars of a nation. When these are neglected, ruin will be its lot." The four tenets are defined by Kuan-chung in the following words:

Propriety is "to refrain from doing that which is not correct."

Moral courage is "to be able to desist from selfish deeds."

Purity is "to be free from evil and dirt in one's conduct."

Sense of honor is "to refuse to follow the footsteps of the wrongdoers."

These definitions reveal Kuan-chung's legalistic mentality. Even in the field of ethics he was more concerned with discouraging the wrong than encouraging the good. On the other hand, his theory to strengthen law enforcement with ethical control of conduct proves that he was not at all uneffected by our moralistic traditions.

A modern revival of Kuan-chung's ethical concepts is the famous New Life Movement, founded by Generalissimo Chiang Kai-shek on February 29, 1934. Coming virtually in the footsteps of the Japanese occupation of Manchuria, the movement was designed to brace us against further Japanese aggression by strengthening our spiritual solidarity. A human experiment as unprecedented as it was far-reaching, it was also intended to transform our romantic, philosophic, sometimes poetic but too often irresponsible and unorganized pattern of living into a vigorous, strenuous, puritanic, and purposeful struggle to bring about our national rebirth. Because the four tenets of Kuan-chung were simple and easy to practice for the masses, they were chosen to be the moral program of the movement. Irrespective of actual accomplishments, it was a momentous decision. It marked our determination to experiment on a collective ethical program instead of following the traditional individualistic programs of the Confucian moralists. While it is difficult to ascertain how much of the success of our bitter struggle against Japanese aggression is due to the New Life Movement, it seems evident that from blood and tears and sweat such as we have never shed before we have learned the importance of adhering to *propriety* by "refraining from doing that which is not correct," to *moral courage* by "being able to desist from selfish deeds," to *purity* by "being free from evil and dirt in our conduct," and to the *sense of honor* by "refusing to follow in the footsteps of the wrongdoers."

THE MILITARIST SCHOOL

IX. SUN-WU, CHINA'S GREATEST TEACHER OF WAR

> As an unlucky weapon, war is resorted to only when there is no other way out.
>
> —An old proverb

THE WEST HAS HEARD of Confucius as a great teacher of peace but has seldom heard of a contemporary of his who was a great teacher of war. China has made Confucius immortal because of the good which can come from his teachings. His contemporary, who taught war, did not rate high with us and is consequently little known.

Among the Chinese philosophers, Sun-wu has a unique place all his own. While the rest of our thinkers were more or less dominated by humanistic considerations, he not only refused to be bothered by ethical values but spent all his life studying and philosophizing on the technique of war, with ease and complacence.

Because of his specialization in the art of war, Sun-wu failed to attract much attention from our scholars, and very little was written about him. Our records merely stated that he lived between 722 and 481 B.C. and that he founded China's knowledge on military strategy.

The events of the time probably did as much in developing Sun-wu's militaristic interest as they did in shaping the humanistic thought of Confucius. Between the years 722 and 481 B.C., commonly known as the "Spring-Autumn Period" in our history, 222 wars were fought in China. When the fighting was at its peak, no less than 140 separate states were involved. While the ravages of war inspired Confucius to ponder seriously how to harness human nature and how to harmonize human relationships as a cure for his time and posterity, Sun-wu found them too exciting not to be studied. Thus for centuries China's military men relied on his *Methods of Warfare* as the standard text of their education. As the book consists of thirteen volumes dealing with such streamlined topics as strategy, supplies, attack, topography, timing, combat, organization, maneuverability, incendiary art, spying, and so forth, a good part of it is still fairly up-to-date.

War, to Sun-wu, was a serious matter. It meant life or death to a nation. He did not bother to glorify it. On the contrary, he admitted that it was cruel and bad. For this reason, he advised that war should be entered into only after serious and responsible consideration and that it should be ended in the shortest possible time. Meanwhile, since it was wholly an evil matter, he did not see any reason why tricks, schemes, and other dishonorable means should not be used to help perform a bad deed effectively.

A nation was not fit for war, observed Sun-wu, unless it fulfilled certain conditions, the foremost of which was undivided loyalty to a definite cause by those concerned. I don't think he cared if the cause were totalitarian or democratic. All that he wanted, in his own words, was that the people and the leaders should have the same mind. "Then," he said, "you can march them to death or life and none shall be afraid."

The strength of a cause was important to Sun-wu. What worried him was not how right or just the cause might be but rather how much unity, conviction, and devotion it could actually command. To be sure, righteousness and justice aid the cause. But being in the right is not enough. Not strong by itself, it merely possesses the qualities to be made strong. Therefore, no nation should consider itself mentally or psychologically well prepared even though it thinks it has a more worth-while cause than its opponent unless the very cause it cherishes is made impregnable by actual unity, devotion, and singleness of purpose on the part of both the leaders and the people.

While spiritual solidarity was an essential part of national strength, Sun-wu also added the quality of "undefeatability" as its physical requirement. "Make yourself undefeatable," he counseled, "then await your enemy's vulnerability." There is much wisdom in this seemingly sinister advice. In terms of our present-day affairs, "undefeatability" is a condition resulting from national solidarity and military preparedness while "awaiting the enemy's vulnerability" can be linked with intelligent generalship.

Sun-wu would not trust the fate of any nation to vague promises or guarantees, however solemnly they were made. His only faith was in the real strength of the people, which can be depended upon at all times, be it peace or war. On this subject he indulged in the luxury of philosophic thinking.

Real strength, averred Sun-wu, should possess the quality of "natural permanence," a sort of living vitality which is adjustable to changing times and circumstances and which does not degenerate. This point of view sounded very much like that of Laotzu, whose exposition on Tao has already been discussed in a preceding chapter.

While Laotzu emphasized the importance of following the ways of nature, Sun-wu injected a dynamic essence into it by proposing to incorporate principles of nature with national strength. A naturally strong person need not be afraid to compete with one who is under the influence of drugs. The strength of the former, being natural, will remain with him long after the latter has spent his when the effects of drugs are worn out. Natural strength, therefore, can be depended upon at all times because it is not produced by artificial, involuntary, arbitrary, or compulsory means. It comes from a nation which is socially, physically, and mentally fit. Strength born of a sudden gust of patriotism, anger, or other forms of emotional stimulants cannot last longer than that which produced it. Only that which lives and constitutes a part of the people is real.

In contrast with his philosophy of "real strength" is Sun-wu's matter-of-fact admission that war is selfish. "A good soldier is one who cares for the livelihood of his people and the safety of his nation," he said. Therefore, in prosecuting the war, he advised: "The best way is to take a state whole and the next to it is to take a state broken." By taking a state whole, which implies bloodless conquest, the strength of the victorious is conserved while the undestroyed resources of the victim are further added to the strength of the conqueror. "Use the resources of the occupied country," he remarked cynically, "and take supplies from the enemy."

Speaking as a professional warrior, Sun-wu regarded war as the last and final resort after all peaceful persuasions have failed. In writing of wringing from the enemy maximum concessions with minimum efforts, he described the successive steps leading to the use of arms in the following words:

"The best way is to scheme. The next to it is by diplomacy. Then comes the threat of war. The worst takes place when you are compelled to do the actual fighting."

In actual fighting, Sun-wu thought that surprise, opportunism, and speed should be given the important emphasis. He defined surprise as a sudden move against the enemy when he least expects it. Opportunism was described as a skillful move at the right time calculated to bring great advantages to yourself while inculcating most disastrous effects on the enemy. It also implied willful scheming to produce the kind of opportune moment to fit into the executor's plans.

On the subject of strategy, China's teacher of war spoke of splitting the enemy when he was united, thinning him out when his defense was concentrated, angering him if he was calm, planting overconfidence in his mind to bring forth negligence and disaster, and tempting him with lures by purposely conceding advantages to him and then outmaneuvering him with extreme mobility.

On the necessity of speed, many of our military leaders still remember a famous saying of Sun-wu: "Soldiering values swiftness most. A good army should move like an arrow leaving the bow."

Our soldier-philosopher objected vehemently against recklessness in the prosecution of war. Rated equally important with skillful manipulation of men, equipment, position, and timing is prudence. "If you have ten times as many troops as your opponent, surround him," he advised; "five times, attack him; if you are equal in numbers and superior in fighting power, engage him; otherwise, avoid the conflict."

To make victory doubly sure, China's teacher of war laid down eight more rules consisting of four warnings and four tactical principles. Many of China's warriors have made their names in our military history by following his leads and developing the details to suit their respective problems.

The warnings were: first, to avoid military blunders; second, not to let those who are unfamiliar with the art of war take part in its deliberations; third, to guard against commissioning officers who do not know how to exercise their authority while commanding the troops; and finally, not to let the emperor interfere with the generals in matters of field operations, which, translated into modern terms, seems to advise against interference with the military command by the politicians, in such matters.

The tactical principles were: first, to know when and where to fight successfully as well as when and where not to; second, to know the correct amount of troops needed for a given assignment; third, officers and men must have unity of purpose; and finally, always be ready to strike, but use the right judgment in delivering the blow where and when the enemy least expects it.

Sometimes a general may have learned all the tricks and finer arts of war and yet, in using them, still lose out to the enemy. This happens when he lacks a flexible and resourceful mind. Sun-wu had a philosophical explanation for it, comparing the manipulation of military tactics to the behavior of flowing water. A stream in the mountain has but one purpose in view, to reach the sea. In doing so, it never has a definite plan for itself as to what specific course it is to follow or how much territory it is to traverse. Yet, according to its natural flow, it seeks its outlet by conquering all obstacles in its way. It sets its natural course, builds its natural valley, and achieves its natural goal. Many a mighty river so makes its flexible, adaptable, natural way. A good general, according to Sun-wu, should handle his military knowledge in the same changeable and maneuverable manner as the flowing water riding the "law of gravity."

Today we hear a great deal about military intelligence and fifth-column activities. In the days of Sun-wu they were known simply as the art of spying. War is evil itself, and all dishonorable means are honorable. From the necessity of securing exact and substantial knowledge from the enemy as the basis for military calculation, Sun-wu formulated the following philosophical doctrine on military intelligence:

"Know yourself and know your opponent, and in a hundred battles there shall be a hundred victories."

Sun-wu's justification for spying, put forth some twenty-five hundred years ago or possibly earlier, was as good then as it is now. "War is cruel," observed the philosopher-warrior, "but to lead a nation to war without knowing fully about the enemy is more cruel." The art of spying, speaking philosophically, is to insure against defeat, to guard against blind plunges into meaningless conflicts as well as against hesitation and inaction in face of danger, and to facilitate intelligent prosecution of war. As a necessary instrument to bring victory closer, it is designed to spare the people from suffering any more than they have to.

Sun-wu did not think that you knew your enemy well if you merely had considerable information about him or could draw conclusions from what you already knew of him. Past knowledge, unsound predictions, insufficient up-to-date information could be as dangerous as, or even more dangerous than, not knowing the enemy at all. In emphasizing the importance of exact, complete, and timely information, Sun-wu remarked: "Get it direct from the enemy."

Our warrior-philosopher classified spies into five categories. He called the first group "native spies." They were the people of a country which was about to be conquered or already conquered in part or in whole. They were won over to your side by good treatment accorded them, by your sympathy for their unfulfilled aspirations, by their trust in you as their friend, or by your fanning their grievance to such a feverish point that they considered the satisfaction of their private wishes more important than resisting you. These people, who were your "spies" or "fifth columnists" in fact but not knowing that they were playing the infamous role, could render valuable aid in your war program as well as supply you with useful information.

The second group was known as "inside spies." They were men of importance within the enemy ranks who were on the inside of things. You got hold of them either because they were officers who had an axe to grind on account of having lost their positions or who embraced private grievances against some higher-up men of their country, or because they were greedy enough to take your bribes. These men could be utilized to supply you with inside information or to perform for you certain inside assignments.

The third group was called "spies in reverse." They were sent by the enemy to spy on you, and you, having learned their real status, used them to carry back the kind of information which would very likely mislead the enemy in accordance with your plans. Also, "spies in reverse" were those who were your spies in fact but were unknowingly employed by the enemy.

The fourth group was known as "dumb spies." They were persons who could hardly pass a present-day intelligence test. Fed with some kind of knowledge about yourself, they were subsequently sent to spy on the enemy. Being dumb, chances were that instead of fishing out information from the enemy they would be tricked into giving out information about you. Since the information was "doped" by you already, the "dumb spy" fulfilled his assignment unknowingly.

The last group was classified as "daring spies." They were brave, conscientious, and resourceful persons whose mission was to convince the enemy with false information or to perform dangerous assignments. Today they are identified as propagandists, rumor-manufacturers, saboteurs, and plotters of various kinds.

I have covered only a few of Sun-wu's many shrewd observations and remarks on the intricate art of war. His original book, antiquated as it is, still is fascinating reading. Were it not for the difficulty of the Chinese language, I would go as far as to recommend reading it, for its entertainment value if not for instruction.

BOOK TWO

THE SHIFT TO CONFUCIANISM

X. CH'IN SHIH-HUANG-TI (259–210 B.C.)

CHINA'S FIRST AND LAST EXPERIENCE OF TOTALITARIAN RULE

"NEWLY BORN KITTENS fear not the tigers," says a Chinese proverb. Today human ingenuity is creating power, both human and mechanical, in unprecedented intensity. It is time to reconsider once again whether we shall ever learn to blend basic human values with the uncertainties of modern living.

China tasted the bitter medicine of human organizational power in the form of totalitarian rule as early as the third century B.C. It was our first and last experience.

With the Second World War ended, the totalitarian threat to the free existence of man may be erased. But the problem of coping with the mechanical power of our creation remains. How much desire do we have to protect ourselves from self-destruction? Do we care?

The story of Ch'in Shih-huang-ti is worth telling. Not only did his despotic rule wean our people forever from the "totalitarian way of life," but it also established once for all the inviolability of our individual dignity. In fact, the resultant animosity toward government control has been so strongly developed that even to this day, in spite of many attempts at regulation, the Chinese people remain basically individualistic.

No less important is the effect of Shih-huang-ti's totalitarian rule on China's trend of national thought. Without the least regard for moral restraint, he used treachery, tyranny, fear, and force of arms to crush every independent kingdom on the Chinese continent. Bent on whipping China into one nation, he burned all the writings which did not meet with his approval. As there was little which he did approve, the destruction was nearly fatal to China's philosophic culture. Those who dared dissent or criticize his policies, he summarily arrested and buried alive. Although the reign of terror lasted less than fifteen years, it was enough to leave an indelible mark on the Chinese mind. We saw that unless we cherished more the Confucian teachings of filial piety, faithfulness, charity, and harmonious living, all of our power, ability, and intelligence would only bring the final downfall of humanity instead of delivering us from our own shortcomings.

The rise and fall of Ch'in from obscurity to hegemony over the rest of China and then from hegemony to complete disintegration looks extremely familiar to those of us who have seen powerful nations in modern times, bent on the cultivation of physical power at the expense of basic human values, going through the same process. Among the seven kingdoms which then divided and ruled China, Ch'in seemed most unlikely to emerge a dominant power. Situated in the remote northwest corner of China, somewhere in the present provinces of Shansi and Shensi, and bordering on the barren lands of the Tartars and Huns, she was too far removed from the center of Chinese culture to be considered a civilized country. In diplomatic and military ventures her participation was seldom sought by any of the independent states. She was regarded as "semi-barbarous" and an international outcast inferior to the rest of China in cultural achievements.

Ch'in's unique geographical position, however, gave her

two advantages which were not enjoyed by the other independent kingdoms. As a neighbor of the Tartars and the Huns, her people had long been toughened by their constant campaigns to rid their country of "barbaric marauders." Shunned by the rest of China, her rulers vowed before their ancestral shrine to wipe out the humiliation by intensive national development. While the other independent kingdoms exhausted themselves in continuous wars, Ch'in sent for experts, technicians, and scholars from all parts of China to strengthen her governmental structure, increase her agricultural and industrial output, and prepare herself militarily for the day of final reckoning. By 334 B.C., in spite of counter measures taken by the rival princes of the other six states, Ch'in was so confident of her power that her ruler summoned all of them to meet him at the capital of the emperor of China. The feudal lords who formerly despised her backwardness now feared her might.

The emergence of Ch'in as the dominant power of the Chinese world put an end to the mad scramble for power among the feudal lords. Plagued as if by a nightmare that disturbed their otherwise complacent sleep, they resolved to wipe Ch'in off the map, the earlier the better. Sharing their conviction were some of the wisest scholars of China, who sensed endless misery for our people should Ch'in's military despotism succeed. Among these was Su-ch'in, a cultivated scholar of deep learning, who vowed to destroy the power of Ch'in by hook or crook.

Believing that only by uniting themselves in a defensive alliance could the six kingdoms save their skins, Su-ch'in called on their rulers one after another advocating immediate consummation of a pact for mutual aid. By 333 B.C. a treaty was signed in which the six kingdoms pledged themselves to help each other in the event one of them should be attacked by Ch'in. To insure its faithful and efficient execution, Su-ch'in was appointed prime minister serving the six kingdoms concurrently.

Ch'in was now isolated. To her north and west were the hostile Tartars and Huns. The new allies surrounding her eastern and southern borders formed an arc of steel shutting her tightly within her own confines. A deadly blow it was to her dream of expansion and conquest.

To counteract Su-ch'in's policy of "collective security," Ch'in developed a series of tactics which dwarfed present-day international power politics. To the capitals of the "Allies" her ruler sent his agents with specific instructions to break up unity. Utilizing their individual fear of his power and their mutual jealousy and distrust of each other, he proposed to every one of them separate alliances of nonaggression running spokewise with Ch'in as the center of the axis. The arguments were convincing. Since Ch'in was militarily more powerful than any of them, it would be suicidal for the "Allies" to risk their national existence by depending on the vague promises of aid from one another. Besides, should any one of them adopt a friendly policy toward Ch'in, he would be perfectly willing to reward them with tangible concessions. To encourage the "Allies" to fall in line with him, he would even cede some territory to anyone who accepted his offer. The seed of mutual distrust was sown, to the dismay of Su-ch'in. And Ch'in's power continued to rise.

When Shih-huang-ti succeeded to the throne in 246 B.C., Ch'in was already the undisputed master over the rest of China. What his predecessors had left undone, he now finished in the true style of a masterful intriguer. Giving his neighbors no choice in peaceful living, he either lured them by momentary concessions to co-operate with him, or threatened them with force if they remained aloof. Believing in boring from within, he sent his diplomats and spies to the allied kingdoms to promote dissension within and mutual distrust with one another by means of bribery, assassination, rumor, lies, and whatever practical intrigues served his purpose. When the time was ripe for attack, he adopted a "skip-jump" tactic whereby he would offer to share the victim's territory with another state bordering on the other side who promised to join him in a simultaneous assault, sandwich fashion. By the time what remained of the allies woke up to his treachery, they were already too weak to withstand his crushing blow. Thus in less than five years Shih-huang-ti was able to wipe out every independent kingdom in sight and emerge as the complete master of China in 231 B.C.

Closely following in the footsteps of military conquest came totalitarian rule. To Shih-huang-ti, the rise of his kingdom from insignificance to complete domination of China was a natural outcome of the concentration of power in his hands and the imposition of regimentation on his people. When the whole of China came under his rule, by force of habit he methodically proceeded to stamp out whatever appeared distasteful to him—assuming that every Chinese could be tamed in the same manner in which he had tamed his own subjects. Thus, with the assistance of Li-szu, a disciple of Hsüntzu, whose story was told in Chapter 5, measures strangely resembling the modern version of totalitarianism were imposed on China with ruthless thoroughness and effectiveness.

The first thing to be destroyed was the national consciousness of the conquered people in the six kingdoms. To detach them forever from their former allegiances, he

divided his new empire into thirty-six provinces irrespective of their previous national identities. Lest the people
remember their past and keep on using their respective
languages, he ordered their books and writings confiscated
and burned except those which were kept for record in the
imperial library. Scholars who dared to voice dissent or criticize his policy were summarily arrested and buried alive.
Only books on agriculture, medicine, and other technical
subjects were allowed to be circulated among the people,
and these too were required to be written in the new,
standardized, and much more simplified language invented
by Prime Minister Li-szu. In addition to putting an end
to feudalistic rule and differentiation in languages, he also
standardized weights and measures and sizes of articles of
daily use.

In spite of the ruthlessness with which he carried out
his policy, Shih-huang-ti might yet be praised for his contributions to our national unity were it not for his utter
disregard of the people's lives and happiness. To make his
empire impregnable against internal revolt as well as external invasion, he proceeded simultaneously to disarm the
people and to put them to work on a huge defense project,
the Great Wall of China, which to this day still frightens
many a casual visitor by its tragic monstrosity and awe-
inspiring immensity. All the weapons in the empire, excepting those in the possession of his trusted legions, were
ordered surrendered to him. From the metals thus
scrapped, he built huge statues to commemorate his mar-
tial accomplishments. He calculated that by depriving his
people of their weapons he could make them voluntary
slaves to his will and impotent for revolt.

To fortify his empire against external threat, particularly
from the Tartars and the Huns of the north, Shih-huang-ti

conscripted hundreds of thousands of men from all parts of China to build the Great Wall. Stretching from the shores of the Yellow Sea westward across virtually impassable mountains and horrifying deserts for a distance of nearly two thousand miles, the Great Wall, equipped with lookout towers, supply depots, and fortifications, stood silently as a monument of his terrifying driving power and the despotic enslavement of his people. Guarded by sentries day and night, with fast-riding horsemen maintaining essential communications along a protected path on top of the wall, and with ever-ready signal fires to summon near-by garrisons upon the slightest sign of Tartar marauders, it was in every sense the last word in military fortification of his day. Never did Shih-huang-ti dream that this mightiest fortress, which was to guard his empire for millenniums to come, would only serve to shut the Chinese in instead of to keep the Tartars out.

From the way Shih-huang-ti planned it, however, the Empire of Ch'in should have had every reason to last for a considerable period of time, if not forever. His people not only were completely disarmed but were simultaneously ruled with such ruthlessness and effectiveness that even the slightest sign of revolt could not escape his detection and devastating punishment. Yes, there were hatred and discontent in the people's hearts. But denied means to express their objection, sentiments alone were impotent. While some daring patriots did make several attempts on his life, none were successful. As far as he was concerned, did not the success of his policies and the completion of the Great Wall testify that in spite of what his people might think of him, his will prevailed over them? What else could worry him when he actually had his people in the tight grip of his hand? Yet, notwithstanding his immunity both from internal revolt and external attack, the Empire of Ch'in collapsed like a house of cards in less than fifteen years!

Was it because our people were neither impressed nor proud of his huge and mighty empire? Were they not grateful to him for uprooting feudalism and instituting in its place an efficient administrative system? Were they resentful of the fact that by his unifying their languages and standardizing their weights and measures they were molded into one nation and one people? Neither the military prowess nor the various acts of regimentation and control had any more effect in insuring the life of the empire than the enforced impotency of the people by weakening their capacity to revolt. It was Shih-huang-ti's totalitarian rule, in utter disregard of individual will and human values, which brought about his downfall!

Among China's numerous revolutions which ended many a less potent dynasty, the one that pulverized the "impregnable empire" of Ch'in was the least exacting on the people's resources. Our history records its downfall in these words: "When one man raised a bamboo standard calling for the overthrow of the tyranny, thousands swarmed to his cause." So spontaneous and contagious was the revolution that in less than a year China's strongest regime was torn to pieces by the bare hands of an otherwise totally disarmed and enslaved people. Yes, throughout his life, Ch'in Shih-huang-ti, our first and last exponent of totalitarianism, never once dreamed that it was fundamentally against the law of nature to deprive his people of freedom of choice by bending their will to comply with his and by forcing them to do things which only suited his fancy. Once the people decided to live their life according to their own choice, even the mightiest of empires stood impotent in the face of their weaponless revolt.

Although the tyranny of Shih-huang-ti was liquidated in a shorter time than it took him to rise to power, the effect on the subsequent trend of Chinese thought was as disastrous as it was encouraging. The burning of the books, including the writings of our ancient philosophers, diverted many of our first-rate scholars from creative thinking to exhaustive research in order to restore the lost classics. As late as the nineteenth century, nearly two thousand years afterward, this process of cultural reparation was still going on with painstaking thoroughness.

In addition to convincing our people once for all of the efficacy of benevolent government, Shih-huang-ti's ruthless rule steeled our determination to be ever watchful lest the emergence of another despot scourge our nation again. When in the course of time Confucianism became China's dominant creed and stayed as such for centuries to come, it was not unrelated to our conviction that the emphasis on ethical values is a surer guarantee of human happiness than brutal might.

While the world at large may have succeeded in coping with tyranny born of human regimentation, we have yet to see what we can do to control the force now being unleashed through man's conquest of nature.

XI. HOW CONFUCIANISM CAME TO DOMINATE CHINESE THOUGHT

CHINESE PHILOSOPHY, after going through Ch'in Shih-huang-ti's baptism of fire, headed for an abrupt turn. Gone were the days when the philosophers of different schools vied with one another for fame or the favor of the feudal lords. Instead of blossoming in multiple colors, our flower of philosophy began to lose its dazzling variety. For the last two thousand years, Confucianism alone has dominated Chinese thought. How it came to be our national creed is therefore a story worth telling.

Succeeding Ch'in was the Han dynasty. Founded in 209 B.C. by Emperor Liu Pang, who, like most of China's monarchs, rose from commoner to royalty by way of revolution, the dynasty was greeted with a most profound psychological change which was then taking place in our country. Exhausted by almost seven hundred years of continuous wars, and with the memory of Ch'in's despotic rule still fresh in their minds, the people were sick and tired of fighting. Wanting rest, relaxation, and quietude, the nation drifted into a life of inactivity and ease. For about a hundred years the philosophy of Laotzu rode the wave of popularity. Our people sighed with exquisite satisfaction upon reading his views on "do-nothing-ism," the "let-na-ture-take-its-course theory," "the smartness of being weak and meek," and "the happiness derived from communion with nature." Under the spell of Taoist doctrines, the nation paused for rest and replenished its war-depleted vitality.

Just as a sick person thinks of activities when he is near recovery, so does a nation when its strength begins to pick up. By the second century B.C. China had recovered sufficiently from the ravages of previous wars to indulge in activities once again. She was restless, and her urge to do things became insuppressible.

Wu-ti was then our emperor. Caught in the whirlwind of national restlessness, the ambitious monarch desired a change from Laotzu's "do-nothing-ism." By this time the chief Confucian classics, wiped out of circulation by Shih-huang-ti, had been rediscovered or reclaimed. These were eagerly studied by the scholars. Convinced by the Confucianist teachings, they told of the illustrious rule of the wise emperors of yore who led the people in virtuous living. This entranced Wu-ti. In his eagerness to transform his reign into a Confucianist utopia, he ordered his officials as well as the scholars to submit to him for study such plans as might help him realize his wish. In the course of time, memoranda from all parts of his realm poured into the imperial court. Among them was one submitted by Tung Chung-shu, a learned man of the day, which won the Emperor's approval.

Stressing that only Confucian teachings could inspire people to moral perfection and rulers to virtuous government, Tung proposed to Emperor Wu-ti three specific policies: (1) that all philosophic ideas other than those contained in the Confucian classics henceforth receive no imperial encouragement; (2) that the Confucian "Six Arts," about which I shall explain later, be decreed the standard learning of the land; and (3) that hereafter only those who excelled in Confucian classics be qualified as officials of the realm.

In an imperial edict issued soon afterward, Emperor Wu-ti commanded the nation that it was his desire to put Tung's suggestions into practice. Hardly did he realize that by one stroke of his vermilion pen he had started Confucianism on the way to dominance, affecting the lives and thoughts of our people for centuries to come. By his singling out Confucianism as the most favored learning of the land, other schools of thought were gradually relegated to insignificance until it alone became the national creed of China. By his requirement that all candidates to officialdom pass a series of imperial examinations on Confucian classics, a peculiar form of "government by scholars" was instituted. Not till the turn of the present century was China able to free herself from the rigid ideological and administrative structure imposed on her by the Confucian way of life.

Confucianism, however, did not come to dominate Chinese life by accident. Rooted deeply in our family system and our conception of "heavenly fate," its doctrines embodied the essences of everything that was China. While other schools of thought speculated on one philosophical subject or another, Confucianism dealt with China as one single entity. Thus, in addition to being a system of thought, it was at the same time a galaxy of knowledge accumulated since time immemorial. The Confucian "Six Arts," consisting of ancient poetry, official records of the various dynasties, history, music, ceremonial rituals, and our ancient philosophical work on the doctrine of change, were in reality a testament of our endeavors, experiences, and teachings of moral perfection. This was to the Chinese what the Old Testament was to the Hebrew people.

While the latter testifies to the religious experiences of the Jews, the former is an accounting of our experiments with virtuous living. It was no wonder, therefore, that in preference to others, Confucianism was chosen to be our standard creed.

Visitors from the Occident seldom fail to notice the tremendous prestige enjoyed by men of letters in China. The respect for the scholar is as characteristic of China as the rapidly decreasing illiteracy among the majority of our people. I can still recall the day when my parents sent me to school. For weeks in advance Mother and Father kept telling me that once I entered school I would become a scholar. As such I was to learn reason and exemplary conduct. The importance, dignity, and responsibility of learning was to be my burden which I must shoulder wisely. The day when the school opened, they clothed me in my best gown. Even my maternal grandmother made a special trip to our home to tell me some more about the intelligent use of knowledge. Although I was then only six and could hardly make out what they said, the honor of learning which my elders injected into my mind stayed with me ever after.

The Chinese respect for scholarship is perhaps more serious than the Western respect for the clergy. Not only do we accord special courtesies to scholars in daily life, but also look up to the latter for guidance in personal as well as public affairs. Considering the fact that scholars have been governing China for the last two thousand years, it is only natural that our people follow their leadership as a matter of habit in disregard of consequences.

The influx of Western civilization during the last one hundred years has affected but little the scholars' traditional position of leadership. It was the scholar class that agitated for reform at the end of the Manchu dynasty. Having failed in their objectives, it was again the scholars who led the revolution of 1911 resulting in the establishment of the Chinese Republic. The renaissance movement of 1915, which contributed among other things the use of vernacular language in place of the ancient classical writing, was carried out by the scholars. The present national government of China, founded in 1926 as a result of the Nationalist Revolution, represented the toil, sacrifice, and patriotism of the scholar class. Today the active leaders of China who are shouldering perhaps the heaviest burden in our history are almost without exception "scholars" of one sort or another. Although the behavior of some of our modern men of letters may not be altogether exemplary, yet as far as China is concerned, they have the destiny of our country in their hands. Hence, for those who seek to understand China as well as to follow the events to come, this rocklike tradition of government by scholars, with its weakness and strength, deserves examination.

Since the dawn of our history we have not known anyone else but the scholars as our rulers. Throughout our national existence, from Confucius to Hu Shih, the voice of the scholar was heard above the grunt of the farmer, the rapid breathing of the laborer, the cry of the hungry, and the plea of the destitute. Not that we were unmindful of the realities of life, but being mindful, we entrusted our happiness to the wisdom of the scholar, whose deep learning should qualify him for leadership. Already a tradition during pre-Han days, scholar rule became a national institution when in the second century B.C. Emperor Wu-ti bestowed upon it his imperial blessing, excepting that whereas, before, any learned man was a scholar, now only Confucianists could qualify for the role.

When scholar rule was first instituted by the Han emperors, China was divided into a number of districts comparable to the congressional districts in the United States. Instead of electing representatives from each district, the original Chinese system called for selection of a given quota of eminent scholars from each district to assist His Majesty in his "virtuous rule for the happiness of mankind." Generally speaking, each district was allotted an annual quota of one scholar-selectee for every 200,000 of its population. Where the population was between 100,000 to 200,000, a quota of one scholar-selectee every two years was provided. Should the population in a given district fall below 100,000, it was entitled to send one every three years.

To qualify for the imperial service, it was more important for a candidate to win the respect of his people than to be popular among them. His conduct must be virtuous and his reputation clean. He must be resourceful, capable, and willing to work for the welfare of his people at all times. Even though it might earn him the executioner's sword, he must be unafraid to correct the faults of the emperor. In addition to his moral qualifications, he must also specialize in one or several branches of practical learning such as law, court procedure, literature, military tactics, astronomy, mathematics, and medicine.

Selection was preferred to election because campaigning by the scholar-candidate was considered indecent and in bad taste. Confucian ethical concepts called for humility and modesty. Self-advertisement should never be indulged in by decent people. Thus no matter how anxious a scholar-candidate might have been to serve his emperor, he had to wait to be discovered and appraised by his family head and village elders. If the venerable gentlemen thought well of him, they would recommend him to the county magistrate. The latter, after carefully considering the qualifications of the candidates sent in by the villages under his jurisdiction, was required by law to report his findings to the highest administrative head of the district. At this juncture the final scholar-selectee of the district was decided upon. In due course of time his name would be sent by the district governor to the emperor for approval. If approved, the scholar-selectee would be ordered to proceed to the capital at public expense to face the imperial examination. When found competent, an official position to match his scholarship and character would be assigned him. Should he fail to pass the examination, then the whole process of selection had to be repeated all over again until His Majesty got his man.

Once a scholar joined His Majesty's service, the appointment was for life, subject only to his own good behavior and the personal pleasure of the Son of Heaven. Should he err in his public duties, not only would he be punished but those who had anything to do with his selection, from the village elder to the district governor, would share the same fate. As a peculiar form of "government by representation," the scholar-selectee, instead of voicing the demands and grievances of his "constituents," merely represented them in the actual administration of the affairs of the nation.

Thus from the second century B.C. till the turn of the present century, government "of the emperor, by the scholars, and for the people" remained as China's principal political structure. Whatever changes were made in the interim were of a minor nature. Instead of relying on recommendation as the source of scholar-selectees, competitive examination, open to all the Confucianist scholars of the land, was gradually instituted in order to accord a more equitable opportunity for those who aspired to public service. While the number of scholars so selected and the courses of study required of them might vary from time to time, the topics to be examined never drifted away from the sphere of Confucian classics.

So deeply rooted was the scholar-rule system that when Kublai Khan, the grandson of Genghiz Khan, conquered the Celestial Empire in the thirteenth century, he too was unable to reserve indefinitely for himself and his descendants the prerogative of imperial appointments without examination. In 1314, less than thirty-eight years following the complete conquest of China by the Mongols, scholar rule by competitive examination was restored. The Mongol horsemen, in order to qualify for public office, had to pass the same Confucian examination as the Chinese scholars. The only advantage the conquerors got was to receive an appointment to office one rank higher than either a Chinese or a Caucasian. Incidentally, by requiring the Mongols to study Confucian classics, scholar rule played a not unimportant part in the subsequent assimilation of the alien rulers by China.

Following the fall of the Mongol Empire in the middle of the fourteenth century, a change for the worse took place in our scholar-rule system. Encouraged by the founder of the succeeding Ming dynasty, the so-called "eight-leg" form of writing became the main feature of the competitive examination. Instead of quizzing the candidates, as was done heretofore, on several fields of Confucian learning, the new method only required them to compose an essay in a rigid literary form on some obscure phrase or part of a phrase taken from one of the Confucian classics. Testing one's skill in sentence construction, the "eight-leg system" divided an essay into introduction, development, contrast, and conclusion, each of which consisted of two parallel ideas. Thus, what was before an actual civil service examination now became a puzzle-solving contest.

One often-repeated story was to the effect that the Ming emperor, who was most respectful to scholars on the surface but actually contemptuous of them, nodded his head and smiled while inspecting the examination halls in his capital. No one knew then what he had in his mind. As years rolled by, it was discovered that our scholars, in their eagerness to pass the examinations, had shifted from the study of serious subjects to the mastery of a superficial technique of "eight-legged" essay composition. Spending most of their time in doing this impractical chore, the same scholars who usually led our people both in peace and in revolt became incompetent. Much to our regret, we realized that the Ming emperor, in encouraging this practice, was more interested in the security of the throne than in the welfare of his people. In ironical consistency with his scheme, when the dynasty which he founded was felled in the seventeenth century, it was not the Chinese but the Manchus from outside the Great Wall who did it.

Throughout the two hundred and sixty years of the Manchu Empire, the "eight-legged" essay composition was retained as the standard to measure the qualification of scholars aspiring to enter government service. With the passing of years, our scholar-rulers, sinking deeper and deeper into the mire of superficiality, knew less and less about the essence of Confucianist learning which in itself was already too antiquated to meet the mounting demands of changing times. During the last one hundred years, when the influx of Western civilization was creating a number of serious problems in the life of our nation, many observers attributed the utter impotence of our rulers to the deteriorated form of competitive examination through which they had qualified for office. It was simply impossible, so they argued, to expect scholars who specialized only in a rigid technique of essay composition to be able to take appropriate measures to meet the crisis and to work for the betterment of China and her people.

At the turn of the present century China, realizing the inadequacy of her ancient system of competitive examination as a method of selecting competent officials, finally had it abolished. But the respect for "learning" and the prestige of the "learned" nevertheless lingers on. Today, with already a record of forty years' functioning of westernized education in China, the position of the "student" in the eyes of the people has not differed materially from that of his predecessor, the "scholar" of bygone days.

A number of deep-rooted obsessions which can only be righted with painstaking effort have been formed during the two thousand years of scholar rule. In spite of our partial westernization and the increasing tempo of revolutionization against the old, these traits are still playing an important role in shaping the events of our country. So intimately are they interwoven with the temperament of our people that a reappraisal of their usefulness is urgently needed today, particularly in the light of coming activities in our country following the victorious conclusion of the war.

Our peculiar *respect for learning*, for instance, is a result of scholar rule. As a tradition, it is based on the assumption that wisdom derived from experience of living is the most precious thing in life. And learning, which represents the gist of life's desirable experiences, should deserve our highest esteem. So, since time immemorial China has been adhering doggedly to her conviction that only the learned are fit to rule. As it turns out, it is no wonder that after being nurtured for centuries by our scholar-rulers, our people simply accept it as a matter of fact that learning is omnipotent. To us there is no other purpose in life but that we live to learn and learn to live till mankind as a unit gradually approaches the goal of moral perfection.

Strangely enough, our respect for learning has done more to arrest a well-proportioned development of Chinese civilization than any other single cause. Although throughout our long history academic research was never given specific restrictions, yet intellectual freedom as we know it today has never had a full share in our national growth. China was a land where intellectual freedom existed in every respect except in fact. Who would want to specialize in other fields of learning while only the mastery of Confucian classics could qualify him for office and usher him into riches and fame? As a matter of fact, from the time scholar rule was instituted in the second century B.C., the best minds of China were so completely drawn to the study of Confucian classics that aside from this they scarcely considered any other branches of learning worthy of their attention. As if to make the matter worse, our scholar-rulers, bound unconsciously by their own conviction of the omnipotence of the Confucian classics, successfully cultivated in our people the belief that only those works which explained the meaning of life could be considered as learning and that among these Confucianism alone gave the right version. Thus for the last two thousand years China has been riding on a Confucianist merry-go-round, leaving scientific and technological subjects pitifully neglected and foolishly unattended. Constantly at the mercy of famine, drought, flood, disease, overpopulation, and economic backwardness, our people were given no constructive leadership but the consolation of Confucian fatalism.

Through the neglect of agricultural, industrial, and other technological subjects, not only did our scholars of ambition find all outlets for distinction shut before them except through the Confucian examination, but the very fact that it alone offered them glory, pomp, respectability, and success produced in our people a nation-wide obsession that an academic degree (instead of a firm grasp on knowledge) was omnipotent. So deeply rooted is our faith in scholastic titles that even today it still largely determines a man's station in life.

For almost two thousand years, every family of means in China prepared its sons for the Confusianist examination. In these, which took place once a year at the county seat, every two years at the provincial capital, and every three years at the national capital, a scholar who managed to pass the three grades was awarded by the emperor the degree of *Hsiu-ts'ai* (man of promising talent), *Chü-jen* (man of elevation), and *Chin-shih* (advanced scholar) in succession. Besides, on the basis of the degrees he held, each scholar was assigned a corresponding government position. As time went by, a strong notion that an academic degree was the positive certificate of a man's ability and an irrevocable passport to fame and riches became indelibly fixed in the minds of our people. Supported by the fact that practically without exception anybody who was somebody in our national life invariably held an advanced academic degree, this obsession met with little in our history that would contradict it.

When at the beginning of the present century China

turned toward Western education for the training of her youth, our belief in the omnipotence of degrees was simply without bias transferred from *Hsiu-ts'ai, Chu-jen,* and *Chin-shih* to the modern B.A., M.A., and Ph.D. Unable to free themselves from the popular conviction that an academic degree is the one and only certificate of one's knowledge and ability, our students who come to the United States to study have to concentrate more on winning their diplomas than on learning something practicable and useful in the service of their country and people.

While there are perhaps more able men among persons having academic degrees than among those without, I sympathize with many a young man in China who in spite of his qualifications has to remain in a subordinate position on account of inability to study abroad. What are the chances of advancement for the untitled young men when all the leading positions in government, industries, banking, and commerce have to go to the "titled scholars" returning from America and Europe? Come to think of it, one wonders whether it is a wise policy not to do something about this obsessed respect-for-learning of ours. By overemphasizing scholastic titles, it has certainly encouraged our youths to go after degrees more than actual knowledge useful to them and their country.

Constant discovery of new knowledge adds to the enrichment of human life. As an essential condition to progress, respect for scholarship is a tradition to be treasured by any nation. And yet, reared almost exclusively on this heritage, why is it that China today shows little appreciable advancement from what she was centuries ago?

The answer to this is our extreme authoritarianism. From childhood to manhood, our individuality was entirely merged with the family. Controlled and disciplined severely by our elders, we had no choice of free enterprise or individual initiative. With the mastery of Confucian classics as the only standard of learning, and scholar-ruler the only distinguishable profession, practically all the genius of our land was corralled into the one little corner —the passing of competitive examinations. Of whatever gain there was in our respect for learning, Confucianism and its priest, the scholar-ruler, claimed the lion's share. If only we will broaden the scope to include the study and discovery of knowledge contributing to the enrichment of life as well as to the understanding of the meaning of life, then this precious tradition of ours may yet free us from a hitherto restricted pattern of living and usher us into a new life with unlimited potentialities.

XII. THE BLENDING OF RATIONALISM WITH RELIGIOUS LIVING

MANY AN EMINENT SCHOLAR on China has observed that religion never occupied a serious place in my country. Arguing that throughout the long years of Chinese history, religious strife was as rare as it was abundant in Europe, they held that as a people the Chinese were not religious-minded. This, to my mind, is both a misobservation and a misconception.

The fact is that in China, religion, state, and learning were intimately interwoven into one single unit from the first century B.C. to the turn of the present century. We outdid medieval Europe in the length of time when the state and religion were inseparable; and at the same time the pursuit of learning was also an integral part of our unique national structure. This statement may startle many a student of China. But I shall presently explain.

Although Confucianism, our dominant creed, is not a religion in the sense that Christianity is to the West or Mohammedanism is to the Islamic world, its two-thousand-year hold on China is definitely religious in nature. Our family elders and scholar-rulers saw to it that our people patterned their character, habits, and conduct on Confucian teachings. While other religious sects were seldom persecuted or oppressed, blasphemy against Confucius, his doctrines, and temples was always punishable as a severe crime. The fact that only those who mastered Confucian classics could qualify to rule was a potent force in its long record of dominance over other creeds and faiths.

Indoctrinated almost entirely with the teachings of the Great Sage, it was the scholar-ruler who for two thousand years cultivated in our minds painstakingly and incessantly the dogma that except moral endeavor there was nothing really worth living for. Relying solely on his Confucianist training, he helped preserve to this day the notion that the pursuit of virtuous living is the indestructible and supreme form of learning. It never occurred to him that learning could also be the knowledge of things contributing toward the enrichment of life. Thus, under his tutelage, China came to regard Confucianism as the only field of learning. Gone were the days of Laotzu, Motzu, Hsüntzu, Kuan-chung and other "pre-scholar-rule" philosophers. In their place was a rigid, impersonal, and authoritarian institution which for two thousand years controlled the way of living in China through a "three-in-one" formula—Confucianism as our national creed, Confucianist scholars as our rulers, and Confucianist classics as our only source of knowledge. Thus, from the Han to the end of the Six Dynasties, over nearly a thousand years, our scholars accomplished very little in the direction of constructive philosophic thinking. Whatever learning we did develop revolved invariably around humanistic thought with Confucianism as its main pivot. And in spite of the blossoming of poetry, literature, and painting in the Tang period (618–905 A.D.), China's philosophic sky, save for the shining of one Confucianist star, remained darkened until the neo-Confucianists came to the rescue in the tenth century.

Notwithstanding that we have had our peculiar brand of trinity—the blending of state, religion, and learning in one—many questions concerning the religious life of China still need to be clarified. Why as a whole are the Chinese seemingly indifferent to religion such as is known in the West? Why can different religions exist in China without friction, persecution, or prejudice? Why is one man's faith in a given religion no concern to another? Why may a Chinese Christian embrace the teachings of other religions with the greatest ease of conscience? How can the Chinese live a religious life without the benefit of a full-fledged religion in the Western sense?

The intensive religious life of the scholar of China, not easily noticeable to Occidentals, is the answer to these questions. Reducing religious teachings to simple, essential "truths," the scholar, by virtue of his position of authority and leadership, helped form the attitude of tolerance among the people. This trait, which is still being retained in the daily life of many of our modern scholars, can be traced back to a period in Chinese history approximately from the tenth to the sixteenth century when rationalism was being developed to merge with our Confucianist way of life. Involving one of the high points of Chinese humanistic thought in which the pursuit of virtuous living was transformed into a fervent religion without the notions of the supernatural and the beyond, this phase of neo-Confucianism reflects illuminatingly the religious psychology of the Chinese people.

Although our neo-Confucianists hated to admit it, the development of rationalist thought from the tenth century onward was to a certain extent stimulated by Taoist and Buddhist thinking. Much may have been said against these "inferior teachings" by our Confucian scholars; they nevertheless studied them and secretly admired some of their doctrines. For instance, they more or less agreed with the Taoists that there was a supreme principle or force which prevailed over all things and by which the universe functioned. They also realized that any system of thought which was derived from this supreme principle or force would be the absolute truth. Where they did not agree with the Taoists was in believing that moral values, instead of Tao, originated from the supreme principle. Thus, from the tenth century onward, volume after volume was written by our neo-Confucianists asserting that from the beginning of the beginning to time everlasting, moral values had been supreme with men as the "all-highest" principle is with the universe. And the Confucian doctrines which embodied the truths of virtuous living should therefore be accepted as in harmony and oneness with the supreme force that founded heaven and earth. This new development, injecting as it did a strong religious element into the Confucian code of ethics, released tremendous influences germinating inspiration, belief, reverence, and even fanaticism within the individual Confucianist, enabling him to experience religious living without the benefit of a clear-cut religion.

From the Buddhists were adopted the neo-Confucianists' modes of spiritual exercise, consisting of "silent-sitting," introspection, and contemplation. Ordinarily, neither the passive philosophy of the Buddhists nor their strange rituals impressed our scholars. But among certain spiritual "gymnastics" practiced by learned Buddhists, the resort to ch'an-ting or silent-sitting, and the communion with the inner soul via introspection and contemplation seemed complementary to the Confucianists' virtuous living.

A Buddhist way of reckoning with one's inner soul, ch'an-ting calls for complete relaxation of physical and mental activity in order to enable the believer to bathe in supreme nothingness as a means of cleansing the spiritual dirt contracted from earthly contacts. Sitting silently alone, with his legs crossed, hands clasped together, eyes closed, breathing slowly and rhythmically, a devout Buddhist could spend hours with himself experiencing religious exhilaration. While subscribing neither to its particular gestures nor to its soulful usefulness, our scholars did see in it a very good method for spiritual training. Besides providing physical relaxation, silent-sitting enables a person to search for his faults and inner weakness through introspection, and to strengthen his moral fiber and ability to do the good through contemplation. Thus, in the course of time, Buddhist elements such as these were incorporated into the newly found rationalist thought by our neo-Confucianist scholars.

In our search for reasons imbedded in ethical values,

neo-Confucianism is a pleasant departure from the institutional Confucianism of the orthodox brand. No longer
could the dogmatic teachings of the old, reinforced by our
family system and scholar rule, bind the expanding force
of our inquiring minds. We wanted to know why moral
values are essential to human life, how we can see through
human nature and discover its innate goodness, and what
to do with ourselves in the pursuit of virtuous living.

From the scattered sayings of the sage and the various
ancient notes about him, our neo-Confucianist scholars
worked out an elaborate system of thought centering on
virtuous living as the ultimate goal in life. Heretofore our
Confucian classics, like a crumpled garment plastered with
gems of all kinds, provided us only with a disorderly picture of Confucianist thought. The rationalist scholars
straightened up the lines, rearranged the gems into a sys-
tematic design, and presented us with an organized and
analytical study of Confucianism. Claiming that such
Confucianist virtues as charity, righteousness, propriety,
wisdom, and faith came from the same supreme principle
as that which originated Heaven and earth, they transformed what were originally the profound sayings of a
wise observer of human nature into absolute, unalterable,
and eternal truth. No longer was our observation and emu-
lation of a virtuous life merely an ethical desirability; to
the neo-Confucianist it became a Heaven-decreed duty.

Speaking of the rationalist thinkers as a whole, they all
agreed that our supreme purpose in life was to pursue a
virtuous life as morally, intellectually, and physically perfect as humanly possible. Where they differed from one
another was in the question of how to develop our "virtuous path" so that we might live up to the Confucian
ideals. Some favored a psychoanalytical approach concen-

trating on the development of our innate goodness from which was to radiate our virtuous being. Others believed that knowledge to improve our moral stature must come from study, research, and relentless practice. In order that my readers may get a more realistic impression of our rationalist thought, I present in the following pages the philosophies of Chu Hsi (1130–1200 A.D.) and Wang Yangming (1472–1528 A.D.), two eminent "scholars of reason," each outstanding in his field, as typical thinkers of the neo-Confucianist school.

XIII. THE PHILOSOPHY OF CHU HSI
(1130–1200 A.D.)

AUTHOR OF ONE HUNDRED and twenty-one booklets of essays and commentaries on the Confucian classics, and the source of another one hundred and forty booklets of lecture notes compiled by his students, Chu Hsi was undoubtedly one of the most eminent neo-Confucianist scholars China ever had. So profound and exhaustive were his treatises on problems relating to ethical concepts that many of his admirers regarded him as the greatest teacher since Confucius.

The life of Chu Hsi is an interesting example of what a Confucianist scholar can be expected to do in the face of adverse circumstances. Such a behavior pattern, incidentally, casts an illuminating sidelight on some phases of the Chinese way of life. Born in 1130 A.D. in the province of Fukien, our philosopher had to live through one of the worse crises in Chinese history.

At that time most of North China was being overrun by the Chin tribesmen from Manchuria. Two of our ex-emperors and some three thousand of their kinsmen were successively taken captives by the invaders. Our surrender envoy Liu Chia had to commit suicide while negotiating a truce with the alien generals. The imperial court was compelled to flee from the capital city of Kaifeng to the coastal city of Hangchow, where it found a temporary haven. Caught between military unpreparedness and the necessity of inevitable capitulation, the officials were struggling along on a day-to-day basis, grabbing as much as they could for their own financial security. Morale was at a low ebb. And the atmosphere was dark and sullen. Amid these rapidly deteriorating conditions, Chu Hsi was able to think clearly, steer his life on a virtuous course, and came out as the greatest Confucianist teacher of his time.

In the cultivation of a great personality such as that of Chu Hsi, the family teaching of the father, true to Chinese traditions, played an important role. A father, as the Confucian code prescribed, lived for his sons just as much as for his ancestors. To his ancestors he owed the moral duty of living a noble life so as not to disgrace them. To his sons it was his obligation under the Confucian code to teach and train them with vigilance so that the pursuit of virtuous living would be their course in life. Chu Hsi's father did exactly what he was supposed to do. He lived a quiet and studious life away from the turbulent and heartbreaking events at the capital. Aside from pursuing virtuous living, he taught and trained his son in the teachings of the Great Master. Was it not Mencius who as early as the third century B.C. advised us to follow the exemplary conduct of our ancestors when he said, "The ancients, when successful, add benefits to the people; when not successful, improve their moral character to show the world"? Chu Hsi's father was not in a position to serve his country as he would have wanted. Considering himself "unsuccessful," he adjusted his ambition to suit his fate and did the best he could by living an upright life and by bringing up his son in the best of Confucianist traditions.

The father's guidance was short-lived. When Chu Hsi was fourteen, his father died. This, however, did not interfere greatly with the youth's scholastic program. By previous arrangement his father had entrusted the care and training of his son to three trusted friends. So where the father left off, they took over and treated the boy as if he were their own, preparing him for the career of a scholar-ruler. Their labor bore fruit when the youth, at the age of nineteen, successfully passed the final stage of the imperial examination. Thus came the honor of a high academic degree and the Emperor's appointment to an official post. Like many scholars before him, Chu Hsi was now on his way to fame and riches.

By virtue of his intelligence and background, Chu Hsi could have advanced rapidly in his official career. But he chose not to. By placing adherence to his moral convictions above working for his own promotion, he did everything except win recognition from his superiors. His criticism of the government's appeasement policy toward the Chin invaders made many an influential official uncomfortable. Furthermore, his interpretation of Confucian teachings, being a radical departure from the orthodox conceptions, won him more skeptics than converts. To those who disliked him, his evangelic activities provided an inviting ground for censure. In fact, many did accuse him of propagating falsehood contrary to the writings of Confucius. One of his superiors even petitioned the emperor to behead Chu Hsi as a warning to those who dared temper with the classics. Although the petition was not granted, it was enough to bar our young philosopher from chances of advancement.

While opposition to his scholastic activities by his fellow officials continued, Chu Hsi went ahead with his set course of study just the same. There was very little his critics could do to stop him. He was not interested in promotions anyway. Thus, throughout his official career he was content with small assignments. On several occasions he even asked for such posts as would allow him to keep up with his studies. In those days the Chinese imperial government maintained a number of offices known as superintendents of Taoist and Buddhist temples. They were posts of leisure created to accommodate officials on the retired or pension lists. Although young and capable, Chu Hsi was always delighted to receive these appointments. Having virtually nothing to do at these posts, he could well afford to spend his time most profitably with his books and academic friends. Even when opportunities did knock at his door, Chu Hsi forsook them in favor of his moral principles. On more than one occasion the emperor, having heard of his academic fame, summoned him for consultation. Instead of making full use of the opportunity, he invariably succeeded in incurring the displeasure of the emperor by openly criticizing the court's appeasement policy toward the Chin invaders and reminding His Majesty of the importance of virtuous living. Thus for fifty-two long years Chu Hsi stuck to his insignificant posts, writing treatises and lecturing on neo-Confucianism on the side. In 1207 A.D., some seven years following his death, his contribution to Chinese thought was finally recognized by the emperor, who honored the philosopher posthumously with the aristocratic title of duke.

Among the neo-Confucianists, Chu Hsi certainly impressed us most vividly with his individualistic and rationalistic pattern of thought. The down-to-earth wisdom which formerly characterized Confucianist thinking could no longer satisfy him. He wanted to know the meaning of creation, the relation between the individual and the universe, and the methods by which moral perfection was to be achieved. He so convincingly presented his thoughts on these questions that they contributed in no mean degree toward the formation of an individualistic and rationalistic mentality which even today still characterizes the Chinese way of thinking.

Chu Hsi approached his inquiry into the true meaning of life in two steps. First he sought an answer to "why." He wanted to know, for instance, why there should be a world, why there should be human beings, and why there should be matter, living and lifeless, around us. He felt that if he could find the answer, he would be in a position to determine more correctly the purpose of human life. From this point he proceeded to inquire about the "How." He wanted to know, for instance, how this world comes to be what it is, how human beings become what they are, and how all kinds of matter, living and lifeless, come to be what they are. These answers were important to him because he considered them to be the manifestations of the *purpose of creation*. By putting his findings about the purpose of life and about its manifestations together, he arrived at his understanding of the meaning of life.

Chu Hsi believed that the universe came to be what it is by virtue of the presence of the one supreme principle. This he called Li (理), or the *ultimate reason or purpose*. While the one supreme principle constitutes the source of all creation, it does not create things. From the supreme principle are developed two forces, ying, the negative, and yang, the positive. These two forces, possessing physical properties, react toward each other in a number of ways. By this interaction all matter, living and lifeless, is created. And the endless process of creation, involving perpetual reaction and change, is called Chi (氣), or the *activating energy*. Of the two basic elements, Li, the ultimate reason or purpose, is metaphysical, while Chi, the activating energy, is physical. The two combined point the way to the understanding of the meaning of life.

From this basic theory Chu Hsi wove his philosophy of life into a rationalistic and individualistic pattern. According to him the individual, being a part of creation, possessed the same two basic elements as those which brought the universe into existence. To Li, the ultimate reason or purpose, could be traced the origin of our innate goodness. But our innate goodness, like the one supreme principle of creation, was merely present within us. It had to be set in motion by Chi (氣), the activating energy. In the case of the individual, Chi (氣) was represented by our abilities to think, move, feel, and generate desires and emotions. With these as our tools we could develop our inner self, which was identical with the purpose of creation, into concrete reality. In the words of Chu Hsi:

"From the Li (理) within us can be traced the origin of our saintly inclination to be good. And from the human faculties within us are developed all of our earthly wants. Thus, the saints entertain human desires such as hunger and thirst in the same manner that villains can be expected to show such saintly inclination as sympathy.

"The teaching of our Sage is to have Li (理), our saintly inclination within us, to be our master, and to subject our earthly wants to its direction."

On another occasion the philosopher wrote:

"Heaven and Earth * has for its purpose the creation of matter. All matter, including human beings, have in them the same purpose as that of Heaven and Earth. . . . This purpose, to summarize, is Love.

"Love is behind all creation. Were we able to recognize its meaning and keep it, we would be in possession of the source of goodness and the foundation of living."

If a modern interpretation is justifiable, Chu Hsi's dual doctrines of Li (理) and Chi (氣) in so far as they apply to human living may be comparable to enlightenment and enrichment of living. Enlightenment of living, being metaphysical, is based on the presence of the original purpose of creation within men. It may be called inner goodness by the neo-Confucianists or godliness by Christians. It matters little as long as we know, even vaguely, what it is. Enrichment of living, on the other hand, is based on activating energy, involving human capability of physical achievement. This can mean any number of

* A Chinese term referring to the supernatural.

things from technological accomplishment to social harmony. Each alone, however, does not constitute a true understanding of life. Only by blending *Li* and *Chi* together may human existence be placed on a plane of true recognition of the meaning and purpose of creation.

Chu Hsi's rationalistic approach to life was matched by his practical program of personality training and cultivation. To develop the inner goodness within us which he believed to be in oneness with the purpose of creation, he recommended self-discipline and intensive study as means by which we were to reach our objective. Self-discipline is to strengthen the faculties within us, while intensive study is to enrich our knowledge, thereby leading toward a more intimate recognition of our purpose in life. Both being highly individualistic, they undoubtedly exerted considerable influence in the formation of the individualistic mentality of the Chinese.

To train our mind, to strengthen our will, to review our conduct, and to improve our relations with our fellow men are the subject matter within the scope of self-discipline. They could be effectively performed by introspection and silent-sitting, a form of mental gymnastics. Introspecion, according to Chu Hsi, is psychic concentration aimed at reviewing our own behavior patterns. Wrote the philosopher:

"Introspection is most effective when employed quietly. One should with eternal vigilance constantly examine himself. If he finds himself too talkative, he should quiet down. If he is careless, learn to be prudent. If he is too fresh and shallow, balance it with dignity and dependability." Silent-sitting, on the other hand, is a form of mental gymnastics designed to strengthen one's power of self-control. The idea is to give an individual a certain amount of time each day for solitary reflection and meditation. On this subject Chu Hsi wrote:

"Silent-sitting is not the Buddhist type of Ch'an-ting which requires the cessation of all processes of thinking. Mine is to help aim our mind so that it will not be distracted by conflicting streams of thought. When our mind is calm and undisturbed, concentration is a matter of course. Thus whatever may confront us can be handled with ease."

Self-correction through introspection, and psychic stabilization through silent-sitting, while helpful in the pursuit of virtuous living, cannot by themselves guide us to our objective in life. We may liken ourselves to a well-constructed ship equipped with complete instruments—it must have a qualified pilot to take it through thick and thin. This qualified pilot, in the philosophic system of Chu Hsi, is knowledge. Inasmuch as the individual must live with himself, his fellow men, and things around him, he cannot live happily and wisely without a true knowledge of them. Said Chu Hsi:

"What is meant by acquiring knowledge through the study of matter is to investigate intensively every object and to discover general truths therefrom. The human mind possesses the ability to learn. Our knowledge of things can never be complete, because things around us are endless sources of truths."

If knowledge, as conceived by Chu Hsi, points both toward the acquisition of wisdom for the enlightenment of living and toward discovery of general truths for the enrichment of living, then why is it that the net influence he left behind is still the encouragement among our scholars of an individualistic and rationalistic mentality with little trace of the scientific spirit? Whatever Chu Hsi said and wrote, whether concerning the doctrines of *Li* and *Chi*, introspection, silent-sitting, or intensive study for the acquisition of knowledge, was highly rationalistic and individualistic. To those who came under his influence, his teachings could not but produce an individualistic attempt rationally to pursue what he believed to be the Confucianist way of life. Since problems of ethical conduct are mostly personal, whatever light Chu Hsi may have thrown on the scientific spirit is accidental. Furthermore, because he emphasized time and again the necessity of correlating what one learned from books and the study of objects to actual practice, it is difficult for an average scholar to go beyond the ethical confine and engage himself in the discovery of general truths as the academic world of the West has done. The most that can be said of Chu Hsi is that he was a great ethical thinker who succeeded in presenting the Confucianist program in an organized and logical manner. By so doing, he undoubtedly, for better or worse, helped form our individualistic and rationalistic mentality.

XIV. CHINESE INDIVIDUALISM AC-
CORDING TO WANG YANG-
MING (1472–1528 A.D.)

WERE I ASKED to name a neo-Confucianist thinker whose
influence in the formation of Chinese individualistic mentality exceeds that of Chu Hsi, Wang Yang-ming would be
the man. Instead of depending on subjective introspection
and objective studying as means of character building,
Wang relied solely on the development of one's inborn
goodness. This view necessarily involves intensive individual effort directed toward one's inner self. Being psychic
and almost exclusively introspective, it cannot but produce
a type of personality which is individualistic, self-conscious, sensitive to private virtues, and indifferent to group
activities and public morality. So deeply imbedded in
our minds are some of his views that an understanding of
our mental processes will not be possible without a background knowledge of Wang Yang-ming and his neo-Confucianist thoughts.

The life of Wang Yang-ming, born in 1472 of a scholar-
ruler family in Chekiang Province, differed little from the
lives of his fellow scholars. Any differences which existed
were differences in degree and not in kind. In his childhood days he was known to be unusually bright. Although
he did not speak till he was well over four, he progressed
rapidly once he got started. At ten he was already surpris-
ing his elders with his philosophically worded poems. Like

most Chinese boys from well-to-do families, he did not have to learn to be productive. All he was required to do was to study and recite the classics. This attitude of placing exclusive emphasis on children's intellectual attainments while neglecting other equally important factors in life still persists in Chinese families today. As long as a child proves himself academically proficient, he can get away with nearly anything. As a result, sons from our scholar families are usually intellectually well developed but badly spoiled. And as they grow up, many of them become highly opinionated, critical, non-co-operative, and afraid of hard work. The tragic part of it is that they are more than likely to be the leaders of China.

Wang Yang-ming was, of course, the exception to the rule. But even so, he was rather absent-minded and bookish. He was married at sixteen. But on his wedding day he took a walk and forgot to return for the ceremony. When his uncle found him in a near-by Taoist temple the next day, Wang was still deeply absorbed in a discussion of Taoist mysticism with the priest. Studious both by nature and by habit, he swallowed the contents of any philosophical book within his reach. All these idiosyncrasies notwithstanding, Wang began his official career when he successfully passed the imperial examination at the age of twenty-seven. From then on he divided his time and energy between serving the emperor and following the Confucianist way of life. And the blending of his loyalty to public service with his devotion to Confucianist principles produced an eventful and useful life seldom equaled by scholar-rulers in his time.

At the very outset of his official career Wang's moralistic convictions drew him into open clashes with a corrupt eunuch who was then wielding tremendous influence over the emperor. For this the young philosopher incurred so much imperial displeasure that he was given forty lashes at the court, demoted, and exiled to remote Kweichow. Although Kweichow is now a picturesque and progressive province, in those days it was our version of the czarist Siberia, where in place of extreme cold and desolation one had to live with snakes, wild animals, headhunting tribesmen, and above all, malignant malaria. But the idealistic Wang, rather than compromise his moral convictions, chose the trap of death.

As adversities either break or make a man, Wang's two years of exile were certainly an important factor in his subsequent achievement both as a thinker and as a public administrator. Remembering that true greatness should grow with hardships, our scholar-philosopher faced the terrible environment of his exile with poise, fortitude, and peace of mind. In times of ease, these terms were meaningless. But in the face of loneliness, privation, and despair they became the very instruments that cleansed one's inner self of selfishness and greed, sharpened one's will to resist the evil and to pursue the good, and in his case also provide the foundation upon which he was later to erect his philosophic structure.

Following an imperial reprieve, Wang returned from his exile a confident, wise, and cultivated man fully prepared to face his destiny in life. His subsequent career as a public administrator was marked with success and imperial recognition. For his service in suppressing several rebellions in the empire, he was made a count by the emperor. What distinguished him most was that throughout his busy official career, he never once allowed the duties of state to interfere with his academic activities. Whenever and wherever he found time, he conducted philosophic forums among his friends and established special schools for the study of Confucian way of life. Without exception, he was the moving spirit in these activities, serving as lecturer and teacher.

Wang died young, at the age of fifty-seven, leaving behind him thirty-one booklets of essays and lecture notes on Confucianism—writings which to this day are still treasured and read widely by our high school and college students.

In contrast to Chu Hsi, who held virtuous living to be the outcome of intensive self-discipline and conscientious study, Wang's views came mostly from his own experiences in life. Like all Chinese scholars, Yang-ming spent a good part of his time practicing calligraphy. One day, while looking over his brushwork, he noticed that although in form and construction his style was correct, it showed neither individuality nor life. In an effort to overcome this shortcoming, he came across the words of Chen Ming-dao, an eminent eleventh-century calligraphist and Confucianist scholar, who said: "When I practice my calligraphy, I put my heart into it. Rather than considering it a way to improve my handwriting, I regard it as the proper way to learn." Impressed by these words, Wang realized that while practicing might improve the physical appearance of his handwriting, only by putting his heart into it could he achieve liveliness and individuality. From this he inferred that in emulating the Confucianist way of life, it was the heart behind it, rather than the teachings of it, that counted. Although he was barely eighteen, the importance of intent as a factor in conduct remained a crucial point in his thoughts.

Wang's preference for a spiritual approach to objective study as a practical formula for the pursuit of virtuous living was further influenced by an experiment he made when he was twenty-one. During this period he was reading a number of books written by the rationalist scholars of the Sung dynasty (960–1276 A.D.), who held that the understanding of reason, imbedded in all objects, was the key to true wisdom. Wanting to know just how this could be brought about, he picked his father's bamboo grove as the subject of his study. For three days and nights he sat among the bamboos watching and observing such manifestations of reason as might enrich his knowledge. Instead of achieving any practical results, he contracted a bad cold.

From this lesson, he hastily concluded that when Confucius spoke of studying objects as a source of knowledge, it was meant for the scholar to apply his sense of reasonableness to the objects he was studying. In the case of bamboo, for instance, it offers no reason which will benefit man's moral endeavor. But if one views it as a plant which is humble enough to be hollow inside, hardy enough to stay green the year round, plain enough to adorn itself with slender leaves instead of luxurious blossoms, and dignified enough to stand straight and erect, then one perceives a number of reasons in its worth as a garden companion.

To apply our sense of reasonableness to the problems of life implies that, instead of needing to rely on objective sources for inspirations, the human being is by nature self-sufficient in what is good and virtuous. As long as we are able to project this inborn reasonableness of ours to what we think, say, and do, we cannot but be on the right path. Elaborating this theory, Wang Yang-ming maintained that human conscience embodies the essences of true reasonableness, that our purpose in life is to know our inborn goodness, and that the knowledge thus derived should be combined with action.

To explain Wang Yang-ming's philosophy intelligibly to the Occident, I would like to ask my reader to accept as truths a few of his premises. This is not an unreasonable request. Practically without exception our philosophers have been accustomed to advancing straight assertions and considering them self-evident. And few of us ever became skeptical or were so impolite as to ask for proofs. Wang regarded reasonableness as the essence of nature. It was the one supreme principle that created heaven and earth. Comparable to godliness in Christian theology, Wang believed that reasonableness in its true state was present in every human heart. If we only know how to apply our inborn sense to do the good, our conduct will automatically become virtuous. He said:

"The essence of reason is within our conscience. . . . When applied sympathetically, it is charity. When applied appropriately, it is righteousness. When applied logically, it is rationality. Charity, righteousness, and rationality will be lost to us if they fail to originate from our conscience. . . ."

In response to such speculative reasoning, some of Wang's pupils questioned the philosopher as follows:

Pupil: "When you speak of seeking the supreme good from our own conscience only, do you think that can apply to every problem under heaven?"

Wang: "Conscience is the essence of reason. Are there other good things under heaven which do not originate from the goodness within us?"

Pupil: "There are any number of reasons which explain why we should love our parents, be loyal to our sovereign, be faithful to our friends, and be benevolent to those we govern."

Wang: "Filial piety does not come from your father,

nor do loyalty, faithfulness, and benevolence come outside of your own conscience. . . . Human conscience is the essence of reason. As long as it is not clouded by selfish desires, it retains its reasonableness in its native state. This inborn rationality, when applied to your parents, becomes filial piety; when applied to your sovereign, turns into loyalty; when you are dealing with your friends, becomes faithfulness; and when you are governing your people, becomes benevolence and charity. To fully realize the meaning of life, all we need is to concentrate on our inborn intellect."

Pupil: "If human conscience possesses inborn goodness as well as native capability to do the good, then why can human conduct be wrong?"

Wang: "This depends on our ability to retain our conscience in its native state. We lost it when we allowed it to be contaminated by undesirable human wants."

For no other reason than to follow Wang's thread of thought, let us take for granted that we do possess an inborn intellect or sense to do the good: we will still be out on a limb unless we know what this inborn goodness is and how to find it even though it is within us. On this point, Wang Yang-ming again drew heavily from his own experiences for guidance.

During his exile in Kweichow some of Wang's companions lost their minds, while others fell sick in the unhealthy environment. Wang alone was able to overcome the trials and tribulations. In those days he used to decorate the shabby walls of his broken-down hut with two maxims. One was, "Strengthen the will for moral advancement by eternal vigilance," and the other, "Constant self-improvement by gradual steps." With these admonitions he reminded himself that only a life fortified with magnanimity, fortitude, poise, charity, and a reservoir of knowledge and ability could conquer adversities. As was later proven by his success as a public administrator and his fame as a neo-Confucianist thinker, he did develop moral and intellectual strength from what he called his "innate intellect." There were a number of passages in Wang's writings which defined man's *inborn intellect.* Here are some of them:

"Inborn intellect is the instinctive human sense planted within us by nature. . . ."

"Native intellect is imbedded in one's conscience. Its presence is demonstrated by our instinctive love for our parents and affection for our brothers. . . . When unobstructed by selfish motives, our inborn intellect takes the form of omnipotent love in its outward expression. But with an average person, the presence of selfish motives within him is not unusual. He must therefore recover his original conscience by ridding himself of selfishness. This can be accomplished through the purification of one's intent."

The above definitions are more or less disappointing in that Wang Yang-ming, when referring to man's inborn intellect, failed to differentiate it from such terms as reason, essence of reasonableness, innate goodness, instinctive ability to sense the good, and native capability of doing the good. In all probability these terms were synonymous to him. The reader should not be surprised by Wang's lack of exactness. Until the Western scientific spirit succeeds in penetrating deeper into our minds, the fondness for generality will continue to be a national trait of ours.

What Wang tried to say in the foregoing was that all men were endowed by nature with an inborn intellect; that the inborn intellect was good; and that when this innate goodness was expressed in daily living, the resultant manifestations would also be good. To make sure that our innate good sense alone should guide our daily lives, the philosopher proposed a three-point program comprising the elimination of selfishness which might be clouding our innate goodness, the development of innate goodness itself, and the union of knowledge with deeds.

While lecturing to his pupils one day, Wang remarked: "To eliminate selfish desires, to recognize our inborn good sense, and to develop it to fruition are the essences of true learning."

On the elimination of selfishness, Wang favored a rigid individualistic program of self-discipline. He said: "To restore our conscience to its normal state of pure reason, devoid of any speck of unwanted desires, we must guard ourselves against developing any intent which may germinate evil wishes and be able to overcome such an intent when it begins to sprout. . . ."

For the development of our innate good sense, once it was rid of evil desires, Wang gave this practical advice: "What I consider to be the pursuit of knowledge is to apply my innate good sense to everything that I come in contact with. Projecting the pure reason within me into my daily deeds is the way I discovered my original nature."

Although Wang approached his subject matter almost entirely from a psychic and individualistic point of view, he did realize that all the good thus gained would be of little value unless it was fused with our daily deeds. "The common fault of our scholars nowadays," he wrote, "is that they regard knowledge and practice as two separate things. For this reason," he continued, "I want to fuse knowledge and practice into one entity."

Wang's theory of unifying knowledge with action made

at least two important contributions to China's humanistic thought. To free our innate good sense of interference from unwanted desires, he insisted that the mere emergence of an evil intent was an evil deed in itself. "I want people to realize," he said, "that when even an intent of any kind emerges in their mind, it is an act already." Just as the preventive medicine is aimed at uprooting the causes of diseases, so is Wang's strict interpretation of evil a preventive step to check evil-doing before its actual commitment.

The fusion of knowledge and action into one entity also awakened our scholars to the true responsibility of learning. Because knowledge and action are one and indivisible, no one can be considered learned unless he also practices what he knows. Just as half truth is not the whole truth, so is knowledge incomplete without practice. Unless we project what we know into actual deeds, all that we learned will be a total loss. For the Chinese, who value abstract learning above everything else, to encounter this theory's way of calling them ignorant is tantamount to being struck by sudden lightning from the sky.

Measured against the existing background, Wang's standard of learning is as good today as when he first proposed it. No matter how much we know of fair dealing, justice, permanent peace, promotion of welfare among men, we may as well consider ourselves uneducated unless we translate it into realities. After all, it is difficult to refute the contention that failure to carry out what we know is just as bad as not knowing at all. The enlightenment of life advances only in proportion to the amount of actual good which prevails in our management of human affairs and in our dealings with one another.

The effect of neo-Confucianism on China is no less important than the Renaissance was to European culture. From the tenth to the sixteenth century the practice of teaching pupils as a method of propagating ideals, suspended since the days of Confucius, was revived. Practically every scholar of some learning cultivated his own following by organizing schools and enrolling disciples. Consequently, never had Confucian idealism been so popularly studied as during this period. And the impression and influence wrought on the Chinese mind was as deep as it was widespread. So much so that from that period onward the Chinese family elders adopted the *Four Books*, the basic Confucian classics, as texts in their schools for children. The subsequent generations of literate Chinese, without exception having been taught Confucian ideals exclusively during their formative years, developed an attitude toward life as Confucian as the rationalist scholars could ever have hoped. The net result was the creation of a nation-wide religious regard for virtuous living which to this day constitutes an outstanding national trait of China.

The intensive program of self-discipline and training developed by the neo-Confucianists also brought into existence a peculiar kind of Chinese individualism which, when analyzed against the present background, may be considered both our strength and our weakness. On our asset side, we developed a kind of religious self-sufficiency by blending reason with moralistic living. While it may not be deemed perfect, much can be said in its favor. The stringent requirements of individual self-discipline brought to crystallization our scrupulous respect for private morality. Because private morality is considered an unmistakable sign of virtuous attainment, we are at times forced to compromise our public duties in the face of personal moral obligations. Thus, while omission of certain public acts may be overlooked, personal ties cannot be lightly dismissed. We are a nation of good individuals but poor citizens. We are able to distinguish ourselves individually, but our record of performance decreases as more persons are required to do a job jointly.

Accent on individual attainment may not be a fatal bar to co-operative enterprises provided we are able to bridge our road to national advancement with the cultivation of social consciousness. Given group training in the ability to do things for ourselves, to co-operate with one another, to organize, to lead, and to follow, I believe that a better national life for China can yet be evolved. In this connection the philosophy of Sun Yat-sen, to be discussed presently, is important.

BOOK THREE

THE BEGINNING OF A NEW ERA

XV. THE EFFECT OF THE MANCHU CONQUEST ON CHINESE THOUGHT

THUS FAR my narrative of Chinese thought has reached sixteenth-century neo-Confucianism. Our next stop will be Sun-Yat-sen-ism, bringing China abreast with the thought of the contemporary world. In the interval, what of importance had taken place?

The year 1644 witnessed the completion of the conquest of China by the Manchus. The alien domination resulting therefrom influenced in several ways the shape of China's thought development. Being foreigners, our conquerors were apprehensive—lest the Chinese who constituted the bulk of the population revolt against them. This meant that measures must be devised to control the masses. As the scholar class had been ruling China since time immemorial, entrusted by tradition with indisputable leadership, the Manchus decided that they would be the best means of harnessing the people. For them the Manchu emperors adopted a two-point program. To provide an outlet for scholars who craved wealth and fame, the traditional competitive examination for government service was continued. Lest they prove dangerous to the security of the throne, their mental alertness and general usefulness were purposely corrupted by exclusive emphasis on the art of composing rigid "eight-legged" essays (see Chapter 11, pages 119-20) instead of practical subjects. As the object of the Manchu conquerors was to live off the fat of the land, they cared little what happened to China's national welfare by depriving our people of intelligent leadership. Nor did the majority of the scholars complain about the superficiality of the examination system as long as it continued to be the royal road to officialdom and its implied fame and riches. The Manchus were not very wrong in pursuing this policy. It took more than 250 years of oppression and corruption finally to exhaust the patience of the Chinese people.

The second point in the "scholar-liquidation program" was for the benefit of those who on account of their moral integrity preferred "learning" to an official career under alien rule. To accommodate them, the Manchu emperors initiated a number of "work projects" with attractive pay. These projects included the compilation of a "Dictionary of Rhymes" (佩文韻府) comprising 212 booklets of source material, an "Encyclopedia of Literature" (淵鑑類函) consisting of 450 booklets of source material, a series of "Selections from the Writings of Pre-Ch'in Philosophers" (子史精華) consisting of 160 booklets of source material, a "Dictionary of Ideographs" (康熙字典) approximating the thickness of forty-two booklets of writings, and a "Collection of Writings, Ancient and Modern" (古今圖書集成) consisting of 10,000 booklets of source material. To top them all, the Emperor ordered seven complete libraries to be set up throughout the empire, each library to be equipped with a complete set of some 36,000 books, (四庫全書) and each set to be copied by hand and written in the most rigid style of handwriting. This policy also worked well for the conqueror. For in addition to keeping the scholars busy on nonpolitical subjects, thereby depriving them of the opportunity of engaging in subversive activities, it also won the good will of our people by demonstrating to them the imperial commendation of the Chinese culture.

The "scholars' work project," however, had its beneficial effects on Chinese thought. Not only did it make available to students of Chinese classics valuable source materials, but the process of compilation itself also led to the development of the science of classical research, a unique feature with the Ch'ing dynasty scholars.

Hitherto we had been more or less at a loss to ascertain whether our wise books of ancient times were genuine or forged. Much less could we tell whether during the centuries of intervening years our learned ancestors might not have tinkered with the contents. But as our scholars went to work on these ancient volumes, they discovered among the books bearing the same title many discrepancies and inconsistencies. Then where a given subject matter was discussed in a number of writings attributed to our ancient philosophers, each version would differ from others. This necessitated painstaking and exhaustive research into the authenticity of every word, sentence, paragraph, and chapter of all our classics which we inherited from our ancestors. As the subject matter to be tackled was too vast for any one scholar at any one time, it became the principal concern of the Ch'ing scholars (1644–1911). Today we are deeply indebted to them for their invaluable footnotes, proofs, and citations which they produced in support of their findings.

The Ch'ing period, last of China's twenty-four imperial dynasties, also opened our door to Western trade and influences. Ever since the middle of the nineteenth century, wave after wave of Western cultural impulses had been pounding at the shores of Chinese complacency. It was absurd to assume that thinking Chinese, however few, could long remain content with the work of classical research. Wars which were strange to the Chinese, long accustomed to peaceful ways, were forced upon us by the Western powers. In rapid succession, military defeats clouded the fair name that was China's. Indemnities, cession of territories, and humiliating concessions were exacted from us. Driven to desperation, a number of our scholars began to look into the potency of Western idealism to see if their beloved China, weakened by the Western arms, could find a way to bolster herself against further corrosion.

In the nineties, scores of scholar patriots under the leadership of K'ang Yu-wei and Liang Ch'i-ch'ao, having been sufficiently convinced of the efficacy of Western ways, initiated a reform movement with the object of putting China on her feet. By careful maneuvering they gained the confidence of Emperor Kuang-hsü. In their effort to win over the country at large, they also interpreted certain Western institutions which they wanted to introduce into China as resembling Confucianism. Countless numbers of books and articles were written to prove the similarities between Confucian ideals and the constitutional monarchy and nineteenth-century liberalism of the West. Unfortunately the four-thousand-year-old cultural wall of China was too strong to be a mere "pushover." The reform-conscious scholars failed in their attempt. Emperor Kuang-hsü died a mysterious death. Six reformers lost their heads to the imperial executioner.

The efforts and sacrifices made on behalf of reform, however, were not in vain. They left a deep impression with the Chinese people. Somehow, we came to the realization that for the survival of China we must forsake the old and seek the new. The groundwork for the eventual acceptance of a more liberal and aggressive program was laid. And Dr. Sun Yat-sen, advocating a modern philosophy revolutionary and socialistic in nature, conceived and developed during the most turbulent years in our history, was destined to give the rapidly aging China a new lease on life, or even rejuvenation.

XVI. DR. SUN YAT-SEN, FOUNDER OF THE REPUBLIC OF CHINA

To ACQUAINT YOU with the life of Dr. Sun Yat-sen, let me take you to a private residence in Peking where on March 12, 1925, the father of the Chinese Republic died at the crest of his career. On a mission which would have ended the rule of the war lords and brought unity to China once again, Dr. Sun, lying prostrate on his bed waiting for the last hour to strike, only managed to save enough breath to shout feebly to his followers around him these words: "Peace. . . . Struggle. . . . Save China. . . ."

Ever since he was twenty years old, Dr. Sun had been devoting his life to the cause of building a new China founded on freedom within and equality without. His ideals, which shaped and are still shaping events in our country, deserve an important place in the history of Chinese thought.

He was born in 1866 on a farm near Hsiangshan in the province of Kwangtung. No one would have thought that one day this farm lad was to bring the four-thousand-year-old edifice of Chinese monarchy to total collapse and on the ashes thereof to erect a new China the structure of which was hitherto unknown in the East's ageless experiences. Between 1879 and 1884, Dr. Sun attended schools in Honolulu where his brother lived. To a boy of ordinary caliber such an experience would be merely an accident in his life. But to our budding revolutionist it was an opportunity to learn how America built its democracy and how American idealism had made its phenomenal growth possible.

Upon his return from Honolulu, Dr. Sun entered Queen's College, Hong Kong, and subsequently, in 1892, completed his medical training at Hong Kong Medical College. During this period, besides reading what he wanted to know, he was near enough to China to observe what was going on. While living under British rule, he could also compare realistically the Chinese situation with the British ways of doing things. It was there and then that he made up his mind to be a physician attending exclusively to the ills of his beloved native land. He nursed his determination and sought compatriots to assist him in performing a major operation on our country—the destruction of Chinese monarchy by revolution.

Things in China were getting worse continuously. The West was busily engaged in administering military defeats upon us and was being paid in silver by hundreds of millions of ounces for doing it. The suffering of the people deepened with successive defeats. No relief was in sight. The corrupt officials continued their customary squeeze. In a desperate attempt to save the country from ruin, Dr. Sun, the first Chinese who ever dared raise his voice without an academic degree from the traditional imperial examination, petitioned Li Hung-chang, prime minister and venerable statesman, on "The Road to National Salvation." This memorandum, written a few months prior to the outbreak of Sino-Japanese War of 1894, embodied most of Dr. Sun's fundamental ideals which in the years to follow blossomed forth into what is known today as *San Min Chu I* or *The Three People's Principles*.

At the time when Dr. Sun submitted his famous petition, the several military defeats experienced by China had already taught our scholar-rulers the indisputable armed supremacy of the West. Maintaining that China was ahead of the West in philosophy, literature, humanism, art, and wisdom of living, and deficient in technological advancement, the imperial government had been modernizing its armed forces by building a navy after the British model and an army after the Prussian. It was argued that when we should have succeeded in matching physical power with the West, China would then be free from further molestation and could again resume its ancient carefree life. In contrast to the stand of the Manchu authorities, Dr. Sun maintained that national power was not built on armaments and that what was more important was the ability of a nation to make full use of its material resources, manpower, and productive facilities. Not being an imperial scholar in accordance with the existing standard, his only chance of being heard was to petition the man in power. Thus in his memorandum to Li Hung-chang, he wrote:

"What I consider to be Europe's basis of prosperity and power is not its iron-clad ships, big cannons, strong forts, and efficient armies. What is essential is its ability to develop to the fullest extent its manpower, its farm produce, its material resources, and its ingenuity in maintaining a free flow of commodities. . . .

"If our country is determined to strengthen itself by Western methods, we would indeed be forgetting the roots and chasing after the branches should we continue to rely on military strength while neglecting the above-mentioned four fundamentals. . . ."

Whether or not the memorandum created any impression on the Prime Minister, no one knows. It went unanswered. History, however, tells us that when in 1894 Japan marched into Korea, then a protectorate of China, Li was so confident of China's newly acquired power that he recommended punitive action against the intruder. In the ensuing battle our Western armament, despite our numerical superiority in ships, was torn to pieces by a neighbor who apparently had followed the same course as we did. Thus, something else aside from our lack of military strength must have also gone wrong.

If the ignominious defeat by Japan in 1894 failed to benefit us in any other way, it certainly confirmed for Dr. Sun his belief that China was away past the stage of reform and that nothing short of a revolution would ever put her on her feet again. From that time onward our revolutionist did everything in his power to overthrow the Manchu empire and to build in its place a new China where, as he said in the memorandum, "her people shall find equal opportunities to put their talents to the fullest use, her farms shall be made to produce to their fullest capacity, and her material resources shall be developed for the benefit of all, and the flow of her commodities shall spread to all parts of the country."

Taking advantage of the inability of the Manchu empire to control its subjects overseas, Dr. Sun saw in the Chinese abroad the most abundant reservoir from which to recruit his followers. From 1895 to 1911 he toured the four corners of the earth crusading for his cause. At first he was greeted with indifference. As he kept on campaigning in spite of the cold responses he encountered, our people began to sense the sincerity of his person and the seriousness of his program. And they swarmed to his standard by hundreds of thousands.

In 1896, while carrying his cause to our people in London, Dr. Sun was kidnaped by a Chinese secret agent and confined in the Imperial Legation of China to await transportation to the homeland for decapitation. Although political prisoners were then protected under international law as now, it made little difference to his captors as long as no one else knew of his fate. For twelve days Dr. Sun sought to communicate with the outside world, but without success. One day a chance passer-by happened to pick up a scrap of paper on the sidewalk by the legation. Tossed out by the prisoner some time before, it was a message calling for help. The subsequent leakage of the news shocked the English public so much that the Imperial Minister of China, in an effort to rectify his mistake, had to let his prize prisoner go. It was probably one of the leading cases in history where an otherwise valueless scrap of paper saved a valuable life.

During this period, 1895–1911, Dr. Sun initiated ten successive revolutions in different parts of China. Although all of them were mercilessly crushed by the Manchu officials, each succeeding uprising was invariably an improvement over the previous one. On October 10, 1911, the eleventh revolution, due to a leakage in the plot, broke out ahead of schedule in Wuchang, Hupeh Province. By this time the Mandarins, who were pretty well scared by the revolutions, were at their wits' end. After firing a few shots, the revolutionists discovered with great surprise that they had already put the officials on the run and frightened the local imperial garrison into surrender. Meanwhile the people, having been won over to the revolutionary cause, started spontaneous revolts of their own in many parts of the country. Within less than two months the Manchu emperor, on the advice of Yuan Shih-kai, the imperial prime minister, found it necessary to abdicate the Dragon Throne. So was the Republic of China born.

At the National Assembly of Provincial Representatives, hastily convened to deal with the new situation, Dr. Sun was unanimously elected China's provisional president. On January 1, 1912, he was inaugurated at Nanking.

The speedy success of the Wuchang Revolution of 1911 left most of the conservative forces in North China virtually intact. To win their support, Dr. Sun resigned the presidency in favor of General Yuan Shi-kai, former imperial prime minister and the military and political leader of the North.

The change in presidency, calculated to bring unity between the North and the South, only succeeded in starting a chain of reactionary events against the security of the Republic. With the imperial-minded Yuan in the saddle, Dr. Sun's followers in the government were liquidated one after another. Military governors, swearing allegiance to the new president, were put in control of the provinces. By 1915, Yuan, with the support of his stooges whom he carefully planted throughout the country, maneuvered himself onto the Dragon Throne and was proclaimed emperor.

To knock out the newly founded monarchy, the remnants of Dr. Sun's forces revolted with the support of the people. In eighteen days the imperial regime, painstakingly built up by Yuan, collapsed. This goes to show that even at that time the revolutionary forces led by Dr. Sun, although not yet constructive enough to build a stable nation in place of the old, were already destructive enough to be able to smash all attempts at restoration.

After the overthrow of Yuan, China was not her original self for a long time. The military governors whom he had put in power now found their positions shaky except as they relied on their personal armies. In rapid succession they turned war lords and during the ensuing two decades ravaged and stripped China bare.

In the meantime, finding all he had worked for shattered to pieces by the reactionaries, Dr. Sun retired to his native Kwangtung, seat of the revolution, to prepare for the final reckoning with the tormentors of the republic. In addition to educating the people on the efficacy of democratic rule and the necessity of industrialization, he also reorganized his Kuomintang, the People's Party, into a strong political unit geared for effective revolutionary action. Avoiding his former mistake of soliciting armed support from the various garrisons, he decided to build an absolutely loyal and indoctrinated military organization of his own. It was at this time that General Chiang Kai-shek came to play a decisive role in shaping the destiny of China by heading the Whampoa Military Academy, the graduates of which have been and are the nucleus of our revolutionary arms.

Alarmed by the progress Dr. Sun was making in the

South, the conservative forces of the North, led by Marshal Wu Pei-fu, an old-time scholar, sought to crush the growing revolutionary nationalism by force of arms. Acting under an attractive slogan, "Unify China by Military Measures," he set his warriors on the "warpath." By the fall of 1924 a big-scale civil war was facing China once again. Fortunately, through the timely interference of Marshal Chang Tso-ling's forces from Manchuria, Dr. Sun was able to defeat Wu's program with little bloodshed. The patience of the people who had been suffering all these years from the rampage of civil wars was now exhausted. They became articulate, demanding unification, peace, and strong leadership. The name of Dr. Sun was hailed from one end of China to the other. It seemed that the country was finally ready to receive him.

Exhilarated over the prospect of realizing his lifelong wish, the venerable revolutionist, now fifty-nine years old, journeyed to Peking, the nation's capital. To reconstruct after the shambles left by the civil wars, he proposed to call a national convention of the people's delegates with the dual purpose of ironing out various domestic issues and planning for the realization of democratic rule. And to liberate China from the semicolonial control of the powers, he advocated immediate abolition of unequal treaties.

Hardly did he realize that the hardships and struggles which he had gone through in his life now bore heavily on him. By the time he reached Peking on the eve of 1925, he was a very sick man. Instead of seeing his lifelong dream come true, he passed away on March 12, 1925, shouting feebly to his followers: "Peace. . . . Struggle. . . . save China. . . ."

Dr. Sun died a poor man. But in the eyes of the common people, his life could not have been richer. He left with us a republic, a program of democratization, and the inspiration to carry on.

XVII. SUNYATSENISM, THE BLUE-PRINT OF NEW CHINA

NOT SO MANY OF MY READERS have an opportunity to look into the intricate patterns of Chinese politics at close range. Yet nothing short of a frank presentation of our basic political objectives can bring about a clear understanding of our problems. Otherwise the strife and strains which are bound to take place in China for some time to come will only cloud our views instead of clarifying them. And China will remain, even though unnecessarily, a political myth to the rest of the world.

An attempt to understand political China should begin with Sunyatsenism. It is the architect's design of China-to-be as well as the blueprint of China-in-the-making, which Generalissimo Chiang Kai-shek and his government are committed to carry out. Likened to the democratic writings of the founding fathers of American democracy, Sunyatsenism is to be treated more as the basic principles of the Chinese Republic than as the aspirations of the Kuomintang. Thus, while we may differ with the men in power as to the methods of excuting the blueprint, the Occidental observer should guard himself from confusing Sunyatsenism with the current issues of Kuomintang dictatorship and the democratization of China. As a body of political doctrines, Sunyatsenism has been intimately woven into the recent history of China. Because of the influence it has already had on our people and will undoubtedly continue to have, it is and will be the most important single force molding the present as well as the future of our country.

This statement can be substantiated by a brief summary of China's political history in recent years. The Kuomintang, originally organized by Dr. Sun, has been instrumental in overthrowing the monarchy, destroying the war lords, and unifying the country. In spite of many an inexcusable shortcoming, it has successfully led the nation in the supreme struggle for survival. Today, even as the Japanese menace is removed, it is confronted with many heartaching problems in the way of national rehabilitation and recovery of law and order. In this our tragic, terrifying, and bloodstained struggle for national liberation, Sunyatsenism has been playing a dominant part. It gave birth to the Republic, nursed it, and tutored it during its formative years. The clamor we hear nowadays for an early materialization of constitutional government is more an offspring of Sunyatsenism than an indictment against it. As young China gradually grows of age, she will certainly bear the traits of Sunyatsenism, stamped on her by the guiding hand of the Kuomintang. It is important, therefore, that the more matured democratic West should make an attempt to understand Dr. Sun's teachings. China's hope of ever becoming a democracy depends on her ability to transform his thoughts into reality.

A concise and authoritative outline of Sunyatsenism was given by the Father of the Republic in his last testament to his followers at the time of his death in 1925. It reads:

For forty years, I have devoted myself to the cause of the people's revolution with but one end in view, the elevation of China to a position of freedom and equality among the nations. My experiences during these forty years have firmly convinced me that to attain this goal we must bring about a thorough awakening of our own people and ally ourselves in a common struggle with those peoples of the world who treat us on the basis of equality.

The work of the Revolution is not yet done. Let all my comrades follow my *Plans for National Reconstruction, An Outline of National Reconstruction, Three Principles of the People*, and the *Manifesto* issued by the First National Convention of our Party, and strive on earnestly for their consummation. Above all, our recent declarations in favor of the convocation of the National Convention of People's Delegates and the abolition of unequal treaties should be carried into effect in the shortest possible time. This is my heartfelt charge to you.

Sun Wen

March 11, 1925*

Since Dr. Sun singled out his *Plans for National Reconstruction, An Outline of National Reconstruction, Three Principles of the People*, and the *Manifesto of the First National Convention of the Kuomintang* as the basic designs by which his followers were to build a new China, I shall endeavor to present a brief summary of each as an introduction to the study of Sunyatsenism.

* Original translation is by Frank W. Price with slight alteration by the author.

1 PLANS FOR NATIONAL RECONSTRUCTION

Comprised of *Sun's Theory* published in 1918, *A Program of Industrialization* published in 1921, and *A Guide to Democratic Procedure* published in 1917, these plans were drafted by Dr. Sun to rebuild China psychologically, physically, and socially.

As a mental stimulant to awaken our people from psychological disillusionment, *Sun's Theory* told of our proud past, our present weakness, and how we can restore our national honor by constructive actions. Hitherto, stunned by the overwhelming superiority of Western arms, and disrupted politically and economically by the influx of Western influences, our people had practically lost all faith in things Chinese and had come to accept Western supremacy, lock, stock, and barrel.

A man who drinks brandy as if it were water likes to consider himself superior to the one who downs *kao-liang* as if it were Coca-Cola; even though to enjoy *kao-liang*, the potency of which matches aviation gasoline, a drinker has to have more stamina. I know of an American missionary, born in China, who used to pride himself on his ability to speak Chinese. This went on well enough for him till the day when he lost his ticket on the train. Too excited to explain his predicament to the conductor in Chinese, he poured forth strings of English words. Stunned by the apparent superiority of his passenger, the conductor shouted: "Don't you try to scare me with an Occidental dialect!" There was a time when to be a member of the smart set, the ability to inject a few English words into one's conversation was the minimum requirement. The fad spread so rapidly that even the conservative merchants began to use English for their commercial advertising. Following the old Chinese custom that what was yours was honorable and good and what was mine was humble and cheap, the calling card of one Chinese bond-salesman had on it this English slogan: "Invest your valuable money in my worthless bonds." Caught by the same craze, a Chinese operator of a hamburger stand, in his eagerness to advertise his familiarity with the American dish both in its ingredients and in the methods of cooking, displayed the following sign: "We Use Absolutely American Methodists."

Never had there been a period in our history when our nation was less sure of itself than during the first two decades of the present century. Everything Western was good. Everything Chinese was bad. Realizing that such a state of affairs would be an insurmountable obstacle to our national liberation, Dr. Sun made psychological rehabilitation the first item in his program of reconstruction. In his lectures he told us how we had lost our grip on our national pride, and how it could be re-established by restoring our faith in moral values as taught by our philosophers. Comparing China's ethical culture with Western technology, he contrasted the ease in mastering science and technical skill with the difficulty in the wise use of knowledge for human welfare. For technology can be acquired in a matter of decades, while a great cultural heritage and stamina must come from centuries of wise living and thinking. To belittle our past moral accomplishments and to imitate the West blindly are two fundamental mistakes which we must correct.

Confidence alone is not enough, he knew. Sandwiched as we had been between foreign domination and domestic chaos, we wouldn't know where to begin even if we believed in our ability to save ourselves. To point out the

way, Dr. Sun, in his book *Sun's Theory,* discussed at length
his philosophy of action. Before him many a philosopher
had taught us that it was easy to acquire knowledge but
hard to put it into practice. Even Wang Yang-ming, who
advised us to fuse knowledge and action into one unit, still
put the accent on knowledge. In a country where the majority of the people were illiterate, it was plain that such
philosophical speculations could not hope to stir us to
mass action. And yet nothing short of mass action could
deliver us from national inertia, mental depression, hesitation, and indecisiveness.

To prepare us psychologically for revolutionary action
en masse, Dr. Sun explained that men, literate or otherwise, possessed an instinctive ability to surmount difficulties which obstructed their well-being. We need not wait
to be educated in order to know what we should do. All
that is necessary is for us to take immediate action to accomplish what we want. The worst that can happen to us
is to wait helplessly for the fate to fall. Where there is a
will, there is always a way.

Convinced by his teaching, our people acted under his
leadership. By actions we learned the wisdom of his counsel. Bound tightly by unequal treaties and abused by our
own authorities, what else could we do to break the bondage but by resort to direct action? And as we acted to improve China's chances of national survival, we also learned
to do better in our subsequent struggles.

Today Dr. Sun's theory of action has been substantiated
by the progress we are making in the direction of our national liberation. If and when more and more of our people are taught to do things for themselves, forces of evil
will have less chance of engulfing us than they had in the
immediate past.

Program of Industrialization

Written by Dr. Sun at the conclusion of World War I, *A Program of Industrialization* was to persuade the victorious Allies to employ their overexpanded industrial facilities for the economic development of China. As an important means of bringing about a gradual improvement in the living conditions of our people, it discusses China's industrial problems mainly from a technical point of view. The projects proposed were of such a gigantic scale that Secretary William C. Redfield of the United States Department of Commerce wrote Dr. Sun on May 12, 1919: "It would take billions of dollars to carry out even a small portion of your proposals."

More important than the technical data of his book is the conviction we gained from the Father of the Republic that we must develop our country industrially as a way of further fostering China's political, social, and cultural progress. While it is not our purpose to grow to be an industrial giant, it is our plan to elevate our country from a semi-colonial status to that of a self-respecting partner in the building of a better world order.

As economic factors will undoubtedly play an important role in the postwar period, Dr. Sun's plans, calling for international collaboration in the economic development of China—to which the present government of China is committed—merit careful consideration by the industrially advanced West.

Guide to Democratic Procedure

A Guide to Democratic Procedure is to teach our people how to conduct a meeting, to elect officers. to make a motion, and to adopt a resolution. Virtually a handbook of parliamentary procedure, its importance to China may not easily be appreciated by the peoples of the West who are more or less familiar with the elementary rules of self-government. But to the people of China who for centuries have not known how to organize and to run a public assembly efficiently, a guidebook of this kind is absolutely necessary to prepare us for the democratic way of government. Imagine what kind of a republic it will be if our people do not even know the rudiments of election!

"Although we have well over 400,000,000 people," commented Dr. Sun in the book's preface, "we are like a pan of loose sand." Being accustomed to individualistic living, we never bothered to learn how to co-operate with one another and how to work together for our common good. Individually as hard as each grain of sand, as a nation we are weak and useless for want of coherence. Democratization of China will be a joke until our people learn how to organize. And there is no better way to cultivate it than to teach our people the technique of democratic organization. A people unacquainted with the ways of self-government is easy prey to demagogues and dictators.

2 OUTLINE OF NATIONAL RECONSTRUCTION

First published in 1924, An Outline of National Reconstruction is Dr. Sun's production plan for transforming a feudalistic China into a modern democracy. The process is not only difficult but well-nigh impossible. To change a heavily garmented and opinionated lady into a flashy and streamlined bathing beauty would have been easier.

Before the plan was formulated, Dr. Sun thought that the task of revolution could be completed by evolutionary means. Following the overthrow of the monarchy and the establishment of the Republic in 1912, steps were taken to transplant the Western representative form of government to China. We started with a presidential system some-what after the French model, a cabinet system which supposedly incorporated the best features of the British, and a parliamentary system consisting of a senate and a house of representatives after the American. To our amazement, these same institutions which had worked well for the Occident failed to function for us. Instead of growing to be the nucleus of a Chinese democracy, the Western version of representative government rapidly deteriorated into a tumor on the body politic of China. Before we had time to realize that those who had never known democratic rule could not be expected to manage the affairs of a republic satisfactorily, the war lords, ushered in both by circumstances and necessity, took over the country. For the next two decades they plunged us into a sea of endless civil wars and miseries.

This swift chance for the worse convinced Dr. Sun that democracy can neither be transplanted nor copied, and that if it is to grow at all it must be grown from our own seeds and in our own soil. To make this possible, the war lords must be liquidated by force of arms. Then the people, rid of their tormentors, are to be taught how to exercise their rights of citizenship. Finally, with the support of an intelligent and responsible electorate, a truly effective constitutional government will function in China. Thus, in his *Outline of National Reconstruction*, Dr. Sun prescribed three stages of transition for China—"the Stage of Military Government," "the Stage of Political Tutelage," and finally, "the Stage of Constitutional Government."

In actual practice, while the national awakening of

China has produced the Kuomintang leadership, the poverty and desperation of our people have also provided background for the Communist movement. In addition modern education, increased contact with the West, industrialization, and improved means of communication have done their part in adding volume to the clamor for an early realization of constitutional government. It seems that if and when China has to choose between division and fusion, a safer solution will be evolution through democracy based on nation-wide co-operation, majority rule, and with measures allowing varying degrees of local autonomy.

3 SAN MIN CHU I OR THREE PRINCIPLES OF THE PEOPLE*

San Min Chu I is the most important part of Sunyatsenism. It consists of the principle of Nationalism, the principle of Democracy, and the principle of Livelihood.

As a body of political doctrines, it was designed to insure our national salvation by injecting national consciousness into the minds of our people, to provide a mechanism for equitable government by converting us to democratic rule, and to foster a rising level of living conditions by instituting economic democracy.

Originally a selected collection of Western ideals incorporated into our best traditions and beliefs, *San Min Chu I* has since become the ideological blueprint of New China. Briefly, what do the Three Principles of the People stand for?

* The manuscripts of *San Min Chu I* were completed in 1922, but were subsequently destroyed by gunfire during a sudden rebellion by one of Dr. Sun's military commanders. The book was published two years later in lecture form.

The Principle of Nationalism

The principle of nationalism taught us that in addition to being human beings, we are a nation distinct and different from other nations. Possessed of a history that was glorious and a culture of which we can be justly proud, it is our duty to restore our national entity and to put China on a basis of equality with other nations. Founded on the Confucian tenet "do not do unto others what you do not want others to do unto you," the doctrine further taught us the following principles: (1) to treat the racial minorities within China as our equals; (2) to treat those peoples with whom China maintains relations as equals; (3) to strive continually for the betterment of China's national status; and (4) to resist those who attempt to impose superiority over us.

While the doctrine of nationalism is not new to Occidentals, Dr. Sun was certainly the first person who opened our eyes to its implications. Hitherto the Chinese people had never realized that they were a nation distinct and different from others. Considering ourselves simply as human beings, we had always regarded other peoples in the same way. Seldom did the idea ever occur to us that among human beings there were groups known as nations which engaged in rivalries, oppression, and fighting. To us, as to Confucius, "within four seas, all men are brothers." And the place where we lived was oftener than not identified as "that which is under heaven."

Unfortunately, China's humanistic view of the essential oneness of mankind was regarded as a sign of backwardness by the West. Labeled as a primitive people without the slightest sense of national consciousness, we were considered unfit for the society of nations. Our lot, so our experiences have shown us, is to be oppressed and exploited as an inferior people.

Dr. Sun saw plainly that, caught in the whirlwind of nationalistic expansion of the nineteenth century, to survive we had no other choice but to turn nationalistic. The job of converting a humanistic entity into a nationalistic China was as hard for Dr. Sun as to change the prevailing nationalistic sentiments into a cosmopolitan fraternity is for the world. But through laborious campaigning and tireless teaching, Dr. Sun did it. Out of his principle of nationalism was born the Nationalist movement which has since been writing most of China's recent history.

The Principle of Democracy

To give substance to our traditional democratic spirit, the principle of democracy was to provide us with a working mechanism so that "government of the people, for the people, and by the people" may effectively function in China.

Ever since the fourth century B.C. when Mencius first declared that "the will of the people speaks for the mandate of Heaven," the rulers of China, with a few exceptions, have been persistently observing the doctrine by acting as self-appointed guardians of people's welfare. In actual practice the Chinese "democracy" is an indirect one. Never given a chance to do things for themselves, our people have been more or less subjected to an authoritarian pattern of living. As youngsters in the family, they were taught to listen and obey while the elders did whatever was appropriate for them. Not until they were well advanced in years did responsibility finally fall on their shoulders. Already molded to the specifications of our rigid pattern of traditions, they in turn took care for their youngsters as their elders once took care for them. In villages where self-government was considered fairly well developed, the same arrangement nevertheless prevailed. A group of family heads known as the village elders got together and decided on what they thought would serve the best interests of the entire village. In the counties, the provinces, and the nation, where affairs were too complicated to be managed by "family representation," scholar-rulers, indoctrinated with Confucianist idealism, were put in office. Acting as the people's guardians, they did what they thought was best for their wards. Thus, in spite of centuries of so-called democratic traditions behind us, the actual exercise of democratic rights is still a novelty to our people. For we were given neither the opportunity nor the training to do things for ourselves. What a time of trial it will be when our people, 450,000,000 strong, take the national destiny in their own hands without having first been thoroughly schooled in the art of self-rule!

In addition to acquainting our people with the rights to suffrage, recall, initiative, and referendum as methods by which we are to govern ourselves, Dr. Sun also advocated a five-power constitution for China, combining Western experience with our own political institutions.

Experimenting with political ingenuity, China had in the course of her history perfected a peculiar three-power system of government. By virtue of the heavenly mandate, the emperor was vested with the power to rule. Through his officials this power was carried out in a combination of administrative, legislative, and judicial functions. Then from among his officials was chosen a selected group of examiners who were charged with the exclusive duty of providing virtuous and just administrators for the emperor. Protected from any interference or undue influence in the discharge of their duties, this branch conducted the imperial examinations, as described in an earlier chapter. Lest the officials, of whatever classification, fall short of their duties, another group of independent censors was appointed to exercise the function of control. Responsible only to their own conscience and moral integrity, they impeached relentlessly both the private and public conduct of the officials and indeed of the emperor himself. Although on a number of occasions some of them lost their heads to the imperial executioner for criticizing His Majesty's behavior too mercilessly, the government itself was kept fairly clean by virtue of their loyalty, integrity, fearlessness, and tenacity. Thus, as an unwritten constitution, the Chinese government of the past was organized on a three-power basis—the power to rule including the executive, legislative, and judicial functions; the power to recruit officials; and the power to censor.

In planning the constitutional structure of New China, Dr. Sun believed that since the independent powers of examination and control had functioned so well in the past, we should incorporate them into the modern system of checks and balances which we are to import from the West. Hence it was proposed that our constitution provide not only for separate executive, legislative, and judicial powers but also for our two traditional powers of examination and control as well.

The Organic Law of the Republic of China, promulgated in October of 1928, represented our first attempt to put Dr. Sun's five-power idea into practice. Although the government was then under the exclusive control of the Kuomintang as it is at present, five "independent yuans" were set up to experiment on the division of executive, legislative, judicial, examining, and censoring powers. Just what the future will bring, only time can tell.

The Principle of Livelihood

Among the Three Principles of the People, the one concerning livelihood is considered the most important. Aiming at changing fundamentally the mode of living of the Chinese nation, it seeks to bring about a gradual rise of living conditions among the masses by way of economic democracy.

To convince us of the important relation which the livelihood of the people bears on national progress, Dr. Sun explained that the determining factor in history has always been the way people make their living. And from the adequate solution of this problem is derived a nation's social and cultural advancement.

Familiar as the making of a living is to the West, the significance of Dr. Sun's views was not fully appreciated by the Chinese. Since time immemorial, the scholar-rulers, impregnated with Confucianist ideals, had been persistently pursuing virtuous living as the one and only road to human happiness. While our history was actually shaped by economic forces, our scholar-bureaucrats doggedly held them in harness, regarding such concerns as obstacles in our prescribed course of duplicating the Age of Golden Rule of our ancestors. Not only were the best minds of the country confined in the study of Confucian classics, but those who did produce useful inventions and discoveries were quickly rebuffed as wasting their precious time and energy on "the small tricks of carving worms," a shameful departure from "the Great Learning of the Sages." The toiling masses were pitifully left to themselves, unattended and neglected. Their only chance of getting out of the rut was for their sons to study the Confucian classics, pass the imperial examination, and be scholar-rulers or mandarin-bureaucrats. While the vicious circle rolls on, the wooden plows which tilled the soil of our ancestors are working on our fields today. The junks which plied our waterways in days of yore are doing a good part of our transportation today. We lagged behind not so much because of inability to strive forward as through our unwillingness to admit the people's livelihood as the determining factor in history.

Citing proof after proof, Dr. Sun showed us why adequate solutions to our problems of food, clothing, shelter, and means of communication are essential to our national well-being and cultural progress; how the experiences of the capitalist nations as well as various socialist theories of the West can profit us; and how the government and the people can work together for the promotion of China's economic well-being.

Speaking more specifically about the coming economic pattern of New China, Dr. Sun counseled that we should adopt a middle-of-the-road course somewhere between capitalism and radicalism. He urged that the nation, while encouraging the development of private enterprises, must devise means to prevent them from growing into menacing giants. Industries either having a monopolistic nature or otherwise fundamentally affecting the well-being of the people should be nationalized. In agrarian problems, Dr. Sun's sympathy was entirely with the millions of toiling tenant-farmers. For their welfare he proposed two-way relief: first, to equalize the right to the ownership of land; and secondly, to require the landlords to file with the government the value of their respective holdings so that the state may either tax them proportionately if the declared value is too high or purchase them when the declared value is too low.

In addition to incorporating the basic principles of the people's livelihood into the Draft Constitution of China, the national government, through its Ministry of Economics, National Planning Commission, and National Resources Commission, has been engaged in the preliminary work of developing a balanced economy for China. While the attention of the government is now principally focused on establishing state-managed enterprises, it has also expressed its readiness to encourage private productive efforts. Thus far one of the difficult problems has been how to reconcile the predominant position of personal influence in public affairs with the scrupulous observation of law as a necessary condition to the successful operation of state enterprises. Much therefore will depend on the degree of political maturity of our people as a whole.

4 THE MANIFESTO

Made public in January 1924, when the Kuomintang was cornered in the South without appreciable political power, licking its wounds from previous defeats suffered at the hand of the war lords, and planning for the final reckoning with the enemies of the Republic, the *Manifesto* issued by authority of the First National Convention of the party represented the first bid of Dr. Sun and his followers for the support of the Chinese people since the party's reorganization. Reiterating its firm adherence to the Three Principles of the People, it offered to our people a concrete program of national reconstruction based on the abolition of unequal treaties, full restoration of China's national independence, establishment of county and provincial self-government, freedom of assembly, speech, and conscience, rural rehabilitation, provision of education facilities, constitutional government, and rational economic development. Inasmuch as none of these items had been realized at the time of Dr. Sun's death, the Father of the Republic mentioned the *Manifesto* in his will as a special charge to his followers to carry out the promised reforms. Its subsequent emphasis in our educational program seems to indicate that the Kuomintang is more than ever committed to the fulfillment of its promise, from which was hatched in 1926 the present national government of China.

To have led us out of bewilderment and chaos and to have provided us with a concrete program of national resurgence were among Dr. Sun's invaluable contributions to China. From 1885 to 1925 the founder of the Chinese Republic worked against a background the complexity of which was not equaled anywhere or any time in human history. He saw a self-assured China, broken by the superior military might of Japan and the West, sinking deeper and deeper into the mire of sullenness, desperation, and self-imposed slavishness. By the operation of unequal treaties and the pressure of foreign military, political, and economic intrusions, the government of China had become more an instrument of foreign diplomatic representatives than an agency in the service of its people. Subsisting mainly on foreign influences, the functions of its officials were narrowed down to the slavish routine of serving the imperialistic interests. Cities which boasted of any economic importance were summarily converted into treaty ports, more or less controlled, administered, or garrisoned by foreign powers. Devoted primarily to exploitation and profiteering, they acted more or less as pumping stations draining the wealth from their respective hinterlands. Nowhere were abnormal wealth and dire poverty in such contrast as in these ports of pseudo-prosperity. It was a cruel period during which the share of international justice for China was extremely slim.

In the domestic scene, the plight of the Chinese people was equally bad if not worse. Ravaged by war lords and bandits alike, mistreated and ignored by a corrupt officialdom, demoralized by poverty and opium, we were a people among whom even the more decent were so disillusioned that they no longer cared what was to happen to their beloved land. As with a patient too sick to rally, it was next to the impossible to restore life and vitality to a rapidly dying nation. Yet it was against a background such as this that Dr. Sun delivered us from extinction, gave us hope, and started us on the road to national resurgence.

Long after the present strife and tribulations and chores of rehabilitation shall have passed, Sunyatsenism, the ideals which arrested our national decadence and generated hope and life in our people, will remain the torchlight of China, carrying the fire of our aspirations to its eventual realization!

XVIII. AN APPRAISAL

WHEN THE JAPANESE armed forces in China, after more than eight years of victorious occupation, surrendered to Generalissimo Chiang's representative in Nanking on September 9, 1945, there, behind the desk on which was signed the surrender document, hung a pair of Chinese scrolls. "The work of revolution is not yet done," said the one at the left, while on the right were written these words: "All my comrades must strive on earnestly." These were the words of Dr. Sun Yat-sen, taken from his last testament, charging his followers to fight for the realization of his ideals.

The wireless photograph depicting this scene appeared in the American newspapers the next day. As I read the words on the scrolls which formed the background of the picture, my heart sank and then started to beat rapidly. China is not what she should be. And we of the young generation must pause, reflect, and know our country as she really is. This is the only basis for intelligent and effective action.

To appraise China's present worth and her future potential, one approach is to make an account of Western impressions of us and compare them with our own subjective knowledge of ourselves. It is like measuring the worth of an individual by what others think of him and what he thinks of himself.

In the course of my career as a consular officer during

the last seventeen years, I have studied enough of China, objectively and subjectively, to enable me to form an opinion.

An American who has not been to China is either indifferent, critical, or widely enthusiastic. Indifference is due to lack of interest, and may be ruled out of the present discussion. Being critical indicates an objective appraisal of what one hears and reads about China which one does not like. And wide enthusiasm is formed objectively by what one reads and hears about China which one likes. Whether the enthusiast's ovation or the critic's admonition is well founded or not, the fact is that there exists in the public mind a definite set of impressions concerning China which are based on abstract information but which are real in spite of it. This I call "China in the abstract."

"China in the abstract" represents both hope and fear. When our critics say that China is not as united as she should be, that her economic structure is backward, that her people are illiterate, poor, and disease-ridden, and that she is far short of the standard as a great power, they are not far from being right. These well-founded charges could spell ruin for any nation, and China is no exception. Herein lies our fear. But when our enthusiasts tell us that we are a great nation with ample resources, that our people are peace-loving, hard-working, and full of common sense, and that we are a nation rich in history, philosophy, and art, we cannot but swell our chests and say: "Yes, China has a great future." And even the skeptics have to agree that these facts are as well-founded as our shortcomings. An appraisal based purely on the impressions of those who have not been to China reveals that my country has as much opportunity to demonstrate her worth as there are dangers to hasten her doom.

An American or a European visiting China usually goes through three stages of psychological reactions. On his first visit, before reaching our shores he is full of expectancy and excitement. Upon his initial contact with China, particularly in one of the busy ports along the coast, he will more than likely be disillusioned, disappointed, and even disgusted. The romantic, philosophic, poetic, and artistic China that was in his mind now comes to greet him in the form of scores of sampans scavenging food and leftovers around his ship. So thoroughly has this been practiced that there is no trace of the familiar sea gulls anywhere. Then as he lands, he is met by swarms of working men in rags shouting and begging to carry his baggage or take him somewhere in a ricksha. The sight is pitiful and the turmoil is unbearable. Finally, in contrast to the handsome buildings, wide and clean streets, and neatly clad pedestrians he remembers at home, he sees China's humanity, poorly clad, trudging along our narrow and winding streets. He either feels sorry for our people and becomes contemptuous of China, or he develops a feeling of spitefulness toward China's officialdom for its inexcusable negligence in attending to the wants of the people. He has seen a part of "China in the raw." For in spite of our long history, the toiling masses of China have always been left very much to themselves. Ever since our scholar-rulers were given the virtual monopoly of government in the second century B.C., the people were governed with benevolence in theory while neglected and unattended to in practice. China's teeming millions whom our visitor sees are China in the raw, having been neither subjected to the poetic, artistic, and romantic influences of the Chinese scholar nor corrupted, abused, or regimented for an evil purpose. They are the products of "live and let live." I meet many Americans and Europeans who never recover from these experiences.

Most of China's visitors from abroad, however, succeed in overcoming their initial disappointment. As the visitor sees more and feels more of China, he falls in love with China so deeply and completely that thereafter nothing else can dislodge him from his attachment to this country. To him, China is freedom from hard work, ease, peace of mind, human warmth, a comfortable feeling of being alive, and a wisdom so worldly that it is almost unworldly in the Western sense. He has learned to adjust himself to the problems and tragedies presented by "China in the raw" and has come to appreciate the mellowness of China. An appraisal based on the impressions of those who have been to China reveals that China in the raw, whether it pertains to her industry, public sanitation, public works, material resources, or to her teeming millions, is relatively undeveloped, while her wisdom of living, even though restricted to a narrow circle, has much to be admired.

What others think of China is like the reflection in a mirror. While skillful make-up may improve the general appearance, it cannot hide one's physical defects. If China expects to see a beauty in the mirror, she must be beautiful herself. Here, a subjective appraisal is in order.

To begin with, it is necessary for China to admit that in a nation where the people have not yet taken an active part in the management of its affairs, the quality of its leadership is the determining factor in either its progress or its retrogression. Again, to be realistic, China must also admit that in spite of the Revolution and the influx of Western ideals, her leaders are restricted to the intelligentsia, the modern counterparts of the scholar-rulers. Until such time as our people can take care of themselves, these leaders, for better or worse, have the destiny of China in their hands.

In analyzing the mentality of the Chinese leaders of today, I am prepared to run into difficulties. To my friends in America, I must make it clear that frankness on my part is not to be construed to mean contempt for my own country. And to my friends in China, I must insist that to be critical is not to be disloyal.

The reader will recall that Chinese philosophers, in discussing their theories, usually indulge in straight assertions and general principles, leaving it to the students to work out their own interpretations. These characteristics are especially evident in the Confucian classics. The reader will also remember that the scholars of China have been reading and memorizing the Confucian classics since the second century B.C. when they became the standard texts of the imperial competitive examination. This means that for more than two thousand years our best minds have been drilled and influenced by the logic as well as the teachings of the classics. Therefore, to deny that the way we think and the way we do things have not been affected by our "rich philosophical background" is to say that previous schooling has nothing to do with one's subsequent patterns of thinking and behavior. Unless we are courageous enough to admit it, any attempt at reform will be defeated by our own deficiencies.

It has been said a number of times that China's future is limited because the Chinese often confuse abstraction with realities. Our critics point out that the officials of China are experts at drawing up plans on paper. A great many reforms and projects of one kind or another may be read and heard by the public, but what has been actually carried out is regrettably little. The skeptics say further that many of the leaders in China, like their scholar-ruler predecessors, are opinionated individuals, gifted in talking and reasoning, uncompromising in their views, and unfamiliar with teamwork and co-operation. To them personal considerations outweigh public well-being so much that no matter how good a system is installed, it will clog, slide, and break down.

These shortcomings are as habitual with our leaders as are some of their good qualities. The logic of the Confucian classics by which we have been drilled for the last two thousand years is abstract, vague, unscientific, individualistic, and opinionated. Determined as we are to do away with the faults, they do linger on. But at the same time, our humanistic thought also teaches us diligence, independence of character, respect for the settled order, adherence to moral duty, and esteem for intellectual eminence. These, too, form a part of our background. What is pertinent in our case is a frank recognition of the importance of habit in the fields of thinking and doing things. China stands to profit if our leaders will cultivate habits of thinking scientifically, of working together, and of doing instead of theorizing.

The greatest hope of China is in our people, the eighty-five per cent of us who are farmers, coolies, and artisans. Because for ages they have been esteemed in theory but neglected in practice, they have learned to be self-reliant, patient, resourceful, hard-working, and above all responsible. Unlike our intellectuals, of whom I am one, who did more talking than fighting the Japanese invaders, the people of China bore the brunt. They were the ones who actually wore the Japanese down and made the dream of conquest a boomerang. Immune from indoctrination by virtue of overwhelming illiteracy, they are every inch human beings—independent, industrious, friendly, simple, home-loving, ready to get out of a fight if they can but to stick to it to the end if they must. When these people are given the blessings of democracy, China will surely be a citadel of peace and orderly progress.

At no time has China had conditions so favorable to the building of a real democracy as she has at present. The surrender of Japan has removed the threat to China's independence and the source of interference in our national life. The world will undoubtedly remain at peace for a considerable period of time. Peace may even reign indefinitely if we all work hard enough for it. This means that China can now rebuild her country in an atmosphere of good will and peace of mind. In prewar days each nation was more or less for itself. The war has taught us to work together, and we have all profited by working together. The era of international co-operation has dawned upon mankind. It should accelerate our speed of progress.

Inside China, we are united to a man that there must be no more civil wars, that there must be democracy, that there must be economic development for the well-being of the masses, and that Generalissimo Chiang Kai-shek, who has so successfully led us in war, must lead us in peace. Thus as China cultivates a new habit of scientific thinking instead of vague theorizing, of doing things instead of merely planning on paper and talking about it, and of working together for the public good instead of concentrating on individualistic self-advancement, then our rich philosophic background, so full of wisdom of life and of living, will certainly make its influence felt in our march toward the building of a political, social, and economic democracy of which we can be justly proud.